The Letters of Napoleon to Josephine

The Letters of Napoleon to Josephine
First published 2004 by Ravenhall Books, an imprint of Linden Publishing Limited

British Library Cataloguing in Publication Data

Napoleon, I, Emperor of the French, 1769-1821
The letters of Napoleon to Josephine
1.Napoleon, I, Emperor of the French, 1769-1821 – Correspondence
2.Josephine, Empress, consort of Napoleon I, Emperor of the French, 1763-1814 – Correspondence 3. Empresses - France – Correspondence
4. France - Kings and rulers – Correspondence
I.Title II. Josephine, Empress, consort of Napoleon I, Emperor of the French, 1763-1814
944'.05'0922

ISBN 1 905043 02 3

Ravenhall Books
Linden Publishing Limited
PO Box 357
Welwyn Garden City
AL6 6WJ
United Kingdom

www.ravenhallbooks.com

Publishing History
The letters in this volume were translated by Henry Foljambe Hall (published in 1901 as *Napoleon's Letters to Josephine, 1796-1812*, by J. M. Dent & Co. in London) but they have been edited against the original French to appeal to a modern audience. The explanatory notes have been edited, corrected and augmented and illustrations have been added.

Printed and bound in Great Britain
by Creative Print and Design (Wales), Ebbw Vale.

The Letters of Napoleon to Josephine

Preface by Diana Reid Haig

RAVENHALL BOOKS

An evening at Malmaison in 1800. Hortense, Josephine's daughter, plays the harp for (left to right) Fouché, Berthier, Joseph, Talleyrand (behind the chandelier), Cambacérès and Lebrun.

Contents

Preface	7
Biographical Notes	13
The General	19
The Consul	65
The Emperor	77
Provenance of the Lettters	221
Chronology	222

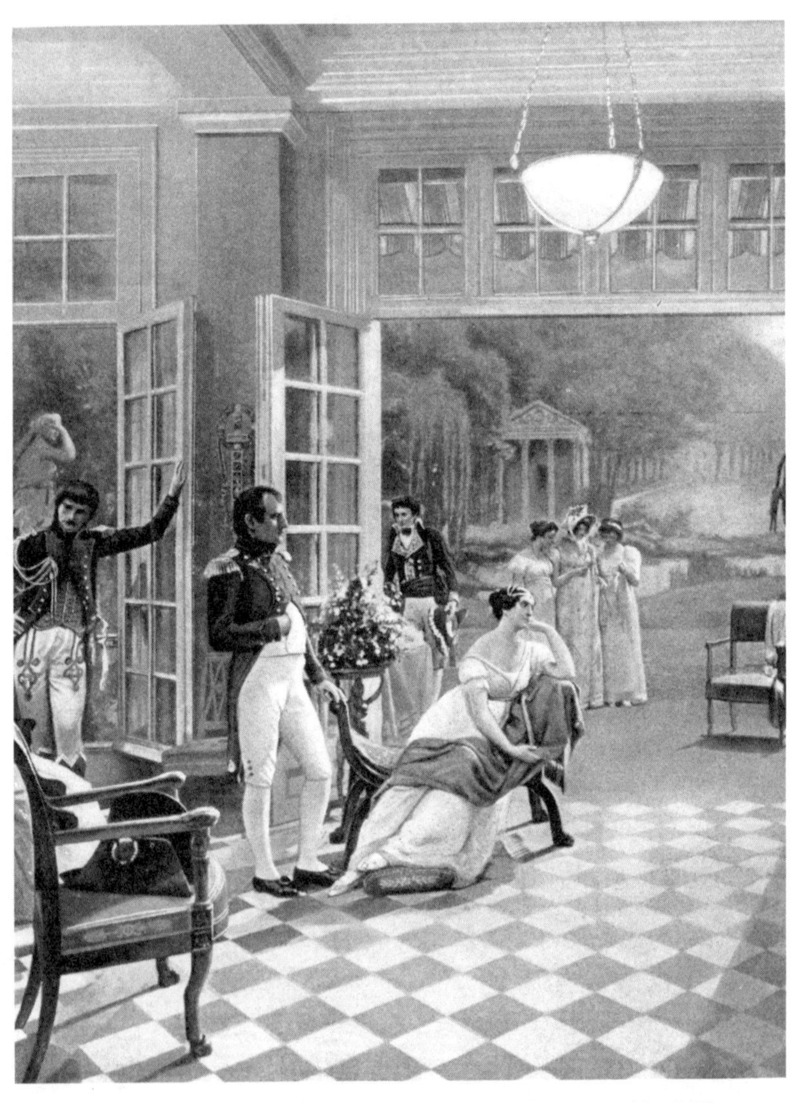

Eugene, Napoleon and Josephine are in the foreground of this scene of family life at Malmaison. Lucien, Mademoiselle Lebrun, Antoinette Auguié and Adèle Auguié are in the background.

Preface

This collection of letters, which spans the years 1796 to 1812, reveals a fascinating portrait of Napoleon and Josephine, one of history's most famous couples. A vivid panorama of their lives unfolds as Bonaparte begins his meteoric rise from gifted young general to First Consul and finally Emperor. Josephine and Napoleon were participants in some of the most colourful events in French history. His victories made them instant celebrities and, for over a decade, they experienced his success together. By 1804, when the Empire was established, they were among the most powerful, glamorous people in Europe.

In an age before telephones and email, people jotted notes to each other constantly. A galloping courier usually delivered Napoleon's letters to Josephine and if the news he carried told of a great victory, he received money or a glittering jewel from the Empress. Napoleon's words to his wife, many of them penned during legendary military campaigns, still thrill today and are considered among the most erotic love letters of all time. Over the course of their thirteen-year marriage, he micro-managed the daily minutiae of their household as well as the most intimate parts of their life. Napoleon also wrote to Josephine about important military events and, as his letters slowly became more formal, the change in his underlying feelings was obvious. His words, while still affectionate, grew careful and calculated. To readers already familiar with this famous correspondence, the explanatory notes provided here offer interesting and often fresh insight into details behind the letters and explain when and why Napoleon is not being honest with his wife.

While the ghostwriter that is the future often haunts biographies and collections of letters, history casts a particularly long shadow over

Napoleon and Josephine. The reader has almost always heard of them and is aware that their story ends sadly. Reading these letters, it is easy to forget that we know more than the person who wrote them about the events to come and what will happen. Napoleon had no such omniscience. Now his divorce from Josephine seems inevitable and his empire doomed, but at the time no one could have predicted the downfall of the man who ruled virtually all Europe. Napoleon, who was superstitious, regarded his elegant wife as his good luck charm and wondered if his lucky star would fade if he left her. Indeed, his reign only lasted four years after their divorce in 1809.

Napoleon met Josephine in the autumn of 1795 as the French Revolution was ending. The 26-year-old general had just come to prominence by successfully quelling a Royalist insurrection in Paris. Although confident in his military abilities, Napoleon was inexperienced with women. Josephine, a widowed former vicomtesse with two children, was his first, and perhaps his only, real love. He later recalled, '... I was not insensible to women's charms, but I was shy with them. [She] was the first to give me confidence.'

Older than Napoleon by six years, Josephine, who did not look her age, was delicate with dark hair and large luminous eyes. Her warmth and radiant presence dazzled him and, as he began escorting her around Paris, he fell hopelessly in love. Even her faults were traits that Napoleon found endearing: she was extremely emotional, bored by books and had no desire to discuss intellectual matters. Josephine was happiest when arranging flowers, doting on her children or shopping for dresses. To Napoleon, she embodied the perfect female. 'She had a certain something which was irresistible,' he later said, 'She was a woman to her very fingertips.'

Josephine was probably the only person who ever truly understood Napoleon – his moods, his restless ambition, his greatness and his passion to leave his mark on history. Although the stylish widow and the gauche young general did not appear to have much in common, they were strangely alike in some important ways. They had both been born on small islands. Napoleon, from Corsica, grew up with Italian as his first language and spoke

French with a heavy accent. Josephine had left her native Martinique in 1779 for an arranged marriage to a young Parisian aristocrat. She called herself a Créole and was proud to be from the Americas. Both Napoleon and Josephine began life in France as outsiders who faced the daunting challenge of assimilating and mastering the intricate etiquette used by the upper class during the last years of the Ancien Régime. Napoleon and Josephine had both known poverty and been imprisoned during the Revolution. Their temperaments also had certain similarities: they were dreamers who were extremely passionate and could charm the opposite sex. Even their names were not the same as the ones they had been given in childhood. Not particularly caring for Josephine's given name of 'Rose', Napoleon asked her to recite her entire maiden name, which was Marie-Josephe-Rose Tascher de la Pagerie. He rechristened her 'Josephine' and, from late 1795, insisted that even her oldest friends address her using this new name. Around the same time, he gallicized his own name from its original Corsican spelling of Napoleone Buonaparte.

Napoleon asked Josephine to marry him in January of 1796 and, although initially reluctant to wed a penniless general, she soon agreed. In March the couple was married in the mayor's office of the 2nd arrondissement. They had known each other just a few months. Two days later Napoleon set out to join the Army of Italy as its new commander while Josephine remained in Paris. His letters to her begin around this time. In his frequent notes, Napoleon pleaded with her to join him and kept her aware of the army's progress. From the beginning his words tumble off the page with a consuming love bordering on obsession. Some passages are so intimate that the reader feels like an intruder viewing confessions that were obviously never meant to be seen by anyone except Josephine. He tells her, 'To live for [you], that is the history of my life,' and adds, 'I hope that before long I shall clasp you in my arms and cover you with a million kisses as hot as if they were from the equator.'

Napoleon swore that he would love Josephine forever. But loving a woman is not the same as understanding her. His bride proved to be an enigma to

Napoleon during the early years of their marriage. The only thing he could be sure of was that he did not resemble the urbane, convivial men whose company Josephine enjoyed. He sadly admitted, 'Nature has not given me attractions with which to captivate you.' Although talk of a divorce came as early as 1799 when he returned from Egypt angry and heartbroken over her public infidelity, it was impossible for him to let her go for another decade. Josephine, adored by the French for her legendary kindness and tact, was in many ways the perfect consort for Napoleon, who was often brusque and blunt. He remarked, 'I only win battles; Josephine wins hearts for me,' and admitted that she exceeded even his expectations of what an Empress should be.

Josephine's feelings for Napoleon began on a much cooler note. Accustomed to the eighteenth-century French practice of arranged marriages, she did not expect conjugal relations to be based on romantic love. When Napoleon wrote her torrid letters, she assumed he was half-kidding and read them to her friends remarking, 'Bonaparte is so amusing'. She could not comprehend that a husband would love a wife with such abandon, found his ardour for her overwhelming and commented, 'He is all day long in adoration before me, as if I were a divinity'.

Napoleon forgave Josephine for her infidelities but she lost his trust. His passion slowly turned into friendship while, sadly, Josephine's feelings blossomed into love and devotion. She became increasingly jealous of his affairs and brooded over her inability to provide her husband with an heir. As the Consulate gave way to the Empire, her infertility became the subject of continual gossip and interest. This was stressful for Josephine, who understood that Napoleon needed to establish a hereditary line, but still hoped that her hold on him would last.

In December of 1809 the couple divorced on friendly terms. Napoleon wanted Josephine to retain the title of Empress and gave her the couple's country home, Malmaison. The Emperor, then 40, quickly married 18-year old Austrian Archduchess Marie Louise, who gave him a son (Napoleon-Francois-Charles-Joseph), the following year. Napoleon named the child the

'King of Rome'. For a brief moment, it seemed as if all his dreams had come true: at last he had a legitimate heir. Soon though Napoleon's ill-advised invasions of Spain and Russia brought his empire to the brink of disaster. The combined armies of England, Prussia, Russia and Sweden invaded France in early 1814 and seized control of Paris. Napoleon abdicated and was sent into exile on Elba, while Marie Louise returned to her father's court in Vienna and took her son with her. Napoleon never saw either of them again.

Josephine died on May 29, 1814 while Napoleon was at Elba. Upon his return to Paris as Emperor during the 100 Days, he asked Josephine's daughter Hortense to meet him at Malmaison where he sadly walked through his first wife's beloved gardens and visited the room where she died. After Napoleon's final defeat at Waterloo in June of 1815, the British held him prisoner on the tiny island of Saint Helena until his death in 1821. Almost twenty years later, his body was returned to France and placed in an elaborate tomb in the Hôtel National des Invalides.

All letters began with a blank page of stationery. Napoleon often wrote on official letterhead. During the early years of his marriage to Josephine, he used the stationery of the *Departement de la Guerre* or the *Armée d'Italie* with the florid banner of the *République Francaise* and the heading *Bonaparte Général en Chef de l'Armée.* For shorter or more personal letters, he sometimes scribbled on small sheets of plain white paper. Most of his voluminous official correspondence was dictated to secretaries, but letters to Josephine (and often those to her children Eugène and Hortense) were hand-written. Napoleon's scrawl was so difficult to read that, early in their marriage, Josephine mistook one of his love letters for a map showing where the army of Italy was bivouacked.

Predictably, Josephine's personal stationery was more elegant. She purchased her writing paper from Susse, the most famous *papetier* in Paris during the early 1800s. Susse (located in the Passage des Panoramas, an enclosed shopping arcade that opened in 1799 and can still be visited in Paris) became an official supplier to the Empress, who ordered stationery and envelopes made of thick crème-coloured vellum with gold or silver etchings on one side. The borders of her stationery featured raised decorative motifs in the style of ancient Rome or Greece. Her letters were sealed with green wax and, after 1804, were monogrammed with the letter 'J' and a small crown.

Diana Reid Haig, 2004

Biographical Notes

Barras, Paul, Vicomte de. 1755-1829. A member of the Jacobin Club who voted for the death of Louis XVI and engineered the fall of Robespierre. He met Napoleon at the siege of Toulon and acted as his patron. After 1795 he was one of the five Directors who ruled France, only being replaced by Napoleon's coup of 18 Brumaire when the General seized control of France.

Beauharnais, Eugène. 1781-1824. Josephine's son by Alexandre de Beauharnais, her first husband. He had a military career and served capably. In 1805 he was made Viceroy of Italy, and was married off to a Bavarian princess. The couple had two sons and three daughters. After the fall of Napoleon in 1814, Eugène retired quietly to some Bavarian estates.

Beauharnais, Hortense. 1783-1837. Josephine's practical and loyal daughter. Married, unhappily, to Louis Bonaparte, she became Queen of Holland in 1806. The couple had three sons but lost their kingdom in 1810. She took a lover, the Count de Flahaut, and had a son by him in 1811. She retired to Switzerland after 1814.

Beauharnais, Josephine (Marie-Josephe, Tascher de la Pagerie). 1763-1814. She was born in Martinique, married Alexandre de Beauharnais and only just made it through the dark days of the Revolution (he didn't and was guillotined). Napoleon and Josephine, who was the rejected mistress of Barras, met in 1795 and were married in 1796 and divorced in 1809.

Bernadotte, Marshal Charles. 1763-1844. Napoleon's difficult Marshal was something of a rival to the Corsican, even marrying Napoleon's rejected fiancée. Bernadotte was later adopted by the Swedish royal family and became King of Sweden.

Berthier, Marshal Alexandre. 1753-1815. Napoleon's hardworking and pedantic chief-of-staff. He died in mysterious circumstances in 1815 or, according to some, simply fell out of a window.

Bertrand, General Henri. 1773-1844. An engineer officer who later accompanied Napoleon into exile on Elba and St Helena.

Bessières, Marshal Jean-Baptiste. 1768-1813. A dashing cavalryman who first served Napoleon as commander of his escort. An important officer in Napoleon's Imperial Guard, this son of a barber amassed a substantial fortune before being killed in Germany in 1813.

Bonaparte, Caroline. 1782-1839. Baptised Maria Annunziata, she changed her name to Caroline and married Murat. She followed him to Naples, proving an effective Queen in that colourful country.

Bonaparte, Elisa. 1777-1820. The eldest of the Bonaparte sisters. She ruled Piombino and Lucca from 1805 and was astute and serious. She was Grand Duchess of Tuscany in 1809 but was deposed in 1814.

Bonaparte, Louis. 1778-1846. Louis served at Napoleon's side from 1794 to 1798. His brother wanted him to marry Hortense de Beauharnais, his step-sister, but he resisted until 1802. The marriage was unhappy. Louis was King of Holland in 1806 and tried to rule after his own fashion. Napoleon objected and Louis abdicated in 1810. He then spent the rest of his time in Italy.

Bonaparte, Lucien. 1775-1840. A wayward member of the Bonaparte clan. More given to writing poetry than ruling nations.

Bonaparte, Joseph. 1768-1844. Napoleon's elder brother should have been a priest but, in an extreme and enforced switch of careers, became a lawyer in Corsica. He married Julie Clary in 1794 and was made King of Naples in 1806. His brother moved him to Spain in 1808, and he abdicated in 1814. He then settled in America, returning to Europe in 1841.

Bonaparte, Jerome. 1784-1860. A great lover of pleasure and the good life, Jerome was denied both by being sent to sea by Napoleon in 1800. He married Elizabeth Patterson in Baltimore much to his brother's chagrin. In 1806 he was given the Kingdom of Westphalia and betrothed to the daughter of the King of Württemberg. He fought at Waterloo.

Bonaparte, Napoleon. 1769-1821. Gunner, General, Consul and Emperor. Napoleon distinguished himself at Toulon. He was given the command of the Army of Italy. From there his rise was meteoric. His career took him to Italy, Egypt, Germany, Austria, Prussia, Poland, Spain, Russia. And, as an afterthought, Elba and St. Helena.

Bonaparte, Pauline. 1780-1825. Napoleon's favourite sister was, by all accounts, beautiful and passionate. Married General Leclerc and accompanied him to Haiti in 1800. He died, she returned and married Prince Camillo Borghese. His fabulous wealth made the marriage a success as did his ability to turn a blind-eye to Pauline's string of notorious affairs.

Carnot, Lazare. 1753-1823. The Organiser of Victory, Carnot played a fundamental role in creating and running the armies of the French Republic. Serving in the Directory for a while before being ousted in 1797, Carnot was an admirer of Napoleon.

Corvisart, Doctor Jean-Nicolas. 1755-1821. Napoleon's favoured doctor. Assisted at the delivery of the emperor's son, the King of Rome.

Davout, Marshal Nicolas. 1770-1823. A superbly efficient soldier who spurned a comfortable life in favour of campaigning. Minister of War in 1815.

Duroc, General Geraud. 1772-1813. An artilleryman who met Napoleon at Toulon. He was Grand Marshal of the Palace in 1805 and an intimate of the Emperor. Killed by a roundshot in Germany in 1813.

Fouché, Joseph. 1763-1820. The arch-intriguer of them all. Minister of Police before being disgraced by Napoleon, Fouché was sent to Illyria but was back in Paris in 1814. He retired to Trieste in 1816 to enjoy his immense fortune.

King of Rome, The. 1811-1832. Napoleon Francois Charles Joseph Bonaparte, i.e. Napoleon's son. Left France when Napoleon abdicated in April 1814 and spent the rest of his life at the Austrian court. Known as Napoleon II, or the Little Eagle, this unfortunate died of tuberculosis at Schoenbrunn, scene of so many of his father's triumphs.

Lannes, Marshal Jean de. 1769-1809. Born in the same year as Napoleon, a trusted General and esteemed Marshal. Victorious in Spain in 1808 and 1809 he died in the 1809 campaign against the Austrians.

Maret, Hugues-Bernard. 1763-1839. Duke of Bassano. Napoleon's first secretary when he became Consul, Maret was an administrator and diplomat of talent. Minister of Foreign Affairs in 1811.

Marie Louise. 1791-1847. Napoleon's second wife was an Austrian Archduchess. She bore him a son in 1811 and the two seemed to be close. However, in 1814, when Napoleon abdicated, she quit France and found love (Neipperg), and a Duchy (Parma), in Italy.

Marmont, Marshal Auguste. 1774-1852. A young artillery officer. Promoted to Marshal by Napoleon he surrendered his troops to the Allies in 1814 and, ever since, was known as Napoleon's betrayer.

Massena, Marshal André. 1758-1817. A soldier with a love for the finer things of life. Given to acquiring them on campaign. Duke of Rivoli, Prince of Essling this old, wily General was showered with honours by Napoleon.

Moreau, General Jean-Victor. 1763-1813. One of the French Republic's best Generals. Napoleon viewed Moreau as a rival and when Moreau was implicated in a Royalist plot, had him banished from France. In 1813 he returned to Europe from exile in the United States and served the Allies as military adviser. He was killed in Germany and buried in Russia.

Murat, Marshal Joachim. 1767-1815. A Gascon cavalryman with a love of theatrical uniforms. Grand Duke of Berg and then King of Naples, he was married to Napoleon's sister Caroline. He was finally ousted from his kingdom by the Austrians and, when attempting to regain his throne with a handful of supporters, was captured and shot by a Neapolitan firing squad.

Ney, Marshal Michel. 1769-1815. Another Marshal born in the same year as Napoleon. A brave soldier he ended his days before a firing squad in the Luxembourg gardens of Paris.

Soult, Marshal Nicolas. 1769-1851. Soult was a talented general and ambitious Marshal. Would-be King of Portugal he was disappointed not to be offered some crown in return for his achievements in Napoleon's armies.

Staël, Madame de. 1766-1817. Novelist, arch-gossip and tourist attraction. Exiled for writing unpleasant things about Napoleon, she was a constant thorn in the Emperor's side.

Talleyrand-Perigord, Charles Maurice de. 1754-1838. Known as Talleyrand. Diplomat, intriguer, survivor. Talleyrand fought on all sides of the Napoleonic era but especially his own. He was supposed to be Napoleon's loyal servant in a number of key aspects of foreign policy.

Walewska, Marie. 1789-1817. Napoleon's Polish mistress she was the wife of Count Walewski. She bore Napoleon a son, Alexandre, in 1810. In 1816 she married Count Philippe-Antoine Ornano, one of Napoleon's cousins, but she died in labour in December 1817 in a house in Paris. Ironically, it was in rue de la Victoire, the street in which Josephine and Napoleon had their first house.

Wurmser, Fieldmarshal Dagobert. 1724-1797. Probably born in Alsace, this soldier spent his life in Austria's service. In July 1796 he was given the task of relieving Mantua in northern Italy and clashed frequently with Napoleon in a series of battles.

The General

General Bonaparte at the battle of Rivoli. A triumphant painting by Philippoteaux to honour one of the young general's many victories in Italy.

It seems likely that Napoleon met Josephine in Paris in September 1795, a precise date has been buried beneath a mass of rumour, romance and speculation. What is known is that Napoleon was fortunate to enjoy the patronage of Barras in 1795 and his circle was dominated by Madame Tallien and a certain Rose de Beauharnais. Rose, known to posterity as Josephine, certainly met Napoleon at Barras' rather unusual salons. By October 28th 1795 Josephine was writing to Napoleon, then the youthful commander-in-chief of the Army of the Interior:

> You no longer come and see that friend of yours who loves you very much; you have abandoned her. You are wrong to do so as she loves you very much. Come tomorrow and lunch with me. I need to see you and discuss your needs.
>
> Goodnight, my friend, I embrace you.

His reply was that 'Had my duties permitted, I would have come in person to deliver this letter'. Duty, however, did not prevent Napoleon from falling in love with Josephine. Napoleon quickly discarded his youthful soulmate, Bernardine Eugénie Clary, known as Désirée, and Josephine managed to rid herself of General Hoche, another talented general who had enjoyed her charms. Napoleon and Josephine's marriage banns were announced on February 7th 1796. They were married on March 9th 1796 in a civil ceremony. Napoleon was two hours late. Josephine declared that she was four years younger than she was, the young Bonaparte 18 months older than was the case. On March 11th, Napoleon set out for Italy, having been appointed commander-in-chief of the Army of Italy on March 2nd. The newlyweds kept in touch, sporadically, by writing.

~ 1 ~

To Madame Beauharnais.

Seven o'clock in the morning.

My waking thoughts are all of you. Your portrait and the remembrance of last night's pleasures have robbed my senses of rest. Sweet and incomparable Josephine, what an extraordinary influence you have over my heart. Are you sulking? Do I see you sad? Are you worried? My soul is broken with grief, and there is no rest for your lover. But is there more for me when, surrendering to the deep feelings which master me, I breathe out upon your lips, upon your heart, a flame which consumes me – ah, it was this past night I realised that your portrait was not you. You leave at noon; I shall see you in three hours. Meanwhile, *mio dolce amor*, accept a thousand kisses , but give me none, for they fire my blood.

N. B.

Napoleon has just been made commander-in-chief of the Army of Italy. Marmont's account is as follows: 'The Directory often discussed with General Bonaparte about the army of Italy, whose general – Schérer – was always complaining that his position was difficult, and never ceased asking for help in men, supplies and money. General Bonaparte showed, in many concise observations, that all that was unnecessary. He condemned the way the victory at Loano had not been exploited, and asserted that it was not too late to do so. Thus a sort of controversy was maintained between Schérer and the Directory, advised and inspired by Bonaparte. At last when Bonaparte drew up plans – afterwards followed – for the invasion of Piedmont, Schérer replied roughly that he who had drawn up the plan of campaign had better come and execute it. They took him at his word, and Bonaparte was named commander of the army of Italy.'

7 a.m. – *Probably written early in March. Leaving Paris on March 11th, Napoleon writes to Letourneur, President of the Directory, of his marriage with the 'citoyenne Tascher Beauharnais', and tells him that he has already asked Barras to inform them of the fact. 'The confidence which the Directory has*

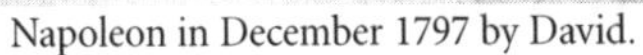

Napoleon in December 1797 by David.

Josephine drawn in 1798 by Isabey.

shown me under all circumstances makes it my duty to keep it advised of all my actions. It is a new link which binds me to the fatherland; it is one more proof of my fixed determination to find safety only in the Republic.'

No 89 of the Correspondence of Napoleon I, *vol.i, this is the last letter signed Buonaparte; after March 24 we only find Bonaparte.*

Accept a thousand kisses. – Un millier de baise (sic).

~ 2 ~

Chanceaux Post House, March 14, 1796.

I wrote to you at Châtillon, and sent you a power of attorney to enable you to receive various sums of money in course of remittance to me. Every moment separates me further from you, my beloved, and every moment I have less energy to exist so far from you. You are the constant object of my thoughts; I exhaust my imagination in thinking of what you are doing. If I see you unhappy, my heart is broken, and my grief grows greater. If you are happy and lively among your friends (male and female), I reproach you with having so soon forgotten the sorrowful separation three days ago; you must be fickle, and unmoved by deep emotions.

So you see I am not easy to satisfy; but, my dear, I have quite different feelings when I fear that your health may be affected, or that you have reason to be annoyed; then I regret the haste with which I was separated from my darling. I feel, in fact, that your natural kindness of heart exists no longer for me, and it is only when I am quite sure you are not cross that I am satisfied. If someone asked me how I slept, I feel that before replying I should have to get a message saying that you had had a good night. The sickness and the passions of men influence me only when I imagine they may affect you, my dear. May my good genius, which has always preserved me in the midst of great dangers, surround you, enfold you, while I will face my fate unguarded. Ah! Be not happy, but a little sad; and especially may your soul be free from worries, as your body from illness: you know what our good Ossian says on this subject. Write to me, dear, and at length, and accept the thousand and one kisses of your most devoted and faithful friend.

This letter is translated from St. Amand's La Citoyenne Bonaparte, *p. 3, 1892.*

Our good Ossian. – *The Italian translation of Ossian by Cesarotti was a masterpiece; better, in fact, than the original. He was a friend of Macpherson, and had learnt English in order to translate his work. Cesarotti lived till an advanced age, and was sought out in his retirement in order to receive honours and pensions from the Emperor Napoleon.*

~ 3 ~

A la citoyenne Bonaparte chez la citoyenne Beauharnais,

Rue Chantereine no. 6, Paris.

Port Maurice, April 3rd.

I have received all your letters, but none has affected me like the last.

How could you think, my love, of writing to me in such terms? Do you believe that my position is not already painful enough without further increasing my regrets and attacking my reason. What eloquence, what feelings you portray; they are of fire, they inflame my poor heart! My unique Josephine, away from you there is no more joy – away from you the world is a wilderness, in which I am alone, and without experiencing the bliss of unburdening my soul. You have robbed me of more than my soul; you are the one and only thought of my life. When I am weary of the worries of my profession, when I doubt the outcome, when men disgust me, when I am ready to curse my life, I put my hand on my beating heart where your portrait is. I look at it, and love is for me complete happiness; and everything laughs for joy, except the time during which I find myself absent from my beloved.

By what art have you learnt how to captivate all my thoughts, to concentrate in yourself my spiritual existence – it is witchcraft, dear love. To live for Josephine, that is the history of my life. I am struggling to get near you, I am dying to be by your side; fool that I am, I fail to realise how far off I am, that lands and provinces separate us. What an age it will be before you read these lines, the weak expressions of a fevered soul in which you reign. Ah, my lovely wife, I don't know what fate awaits me, but if it keeps me much longer from you it will be unbearable – my strength will not last out. There was a time in which I prided myself on my strength, and, sometimes, when casting my eyes on the ills which men might do me, on the fate that destiny might have in store for me, I have gazed steadfastly on the most incredible misfortunes without a frown or a hint of surprise. But today the thought that my Josephine might be ill; and, above all, the cruel, the fatal thought that she might love me less, strikes my soul, freezes my blood, makes me wretched and dejected, without even leaving me the courage of fury and despair. I often used to say that men have no power over the one who dies without regrets; but, today, to die without your love, to die in uncertainty of that, is the torment of hell, it is a lifelike and terrifying figure of absolute annihilation – I feel passion strangling me. My unique companion! You whom fate has destined to walk with me along the painful path of life! The day on which I no longer possess your heart will be that on which nature becomes a cold desert devoid of vegetation. I stop, dear love! My soul is sad, my body tired, my spirit dazed, men trouble me – I ought indeed to detest them; they keep me from my beloved.

I am at Port Maurice, near Oneille; tomorrow I shall be at Albenga. The two armies are moving. We are trying to outwit each other – victory to the most skilful! I am pretty well satisfied with Beaulieu; he needs be a much stronger man than his predecessor to worry me much. I expect I'll give him a good beating. Don't be anxious; love me as you love your eyes, but that is not enough; love me as you love yourself, more than yourself; as your thoughts, your mind, your sight, your all. Dear love, forgive me, I am exhausted; nature is weak for the sensitive, for the one whom you inspire.

N. B.

Kind regards to Barras, Sussi, Madame Tallien; compliments to Madame Château Renard; to Eugène and Hortense best love. Adieu, adieu! I lie down without you, I shall sleep without you; I pray that you'll let me sleep. Many times I shall clasp you in my arms, but, but – it is not you.

Beaulieu. – *The Austrian general commanding in northern Italy.*

Barras. – *Josephine had been the mistress of this member of the Directory. As recently as February 24th she had written to him that she was 'his friend for life'.*

Rue Chantereine no. 6. – *The house Josephine was renting in Paris and which Napoleon first visited on October 15th 1795. In December 1797, in honour of the general's success in Italy, the street was renamed Rue de la Victoire. He purchased the house on March 26th 1798 and the house was renumbered no. 60. He later presented it to one of his generals, Lefebvre-Desnouettes, as a gift. It was demolished in 1857.*

Josephine was renting Rue Chantereine no. 6 for 10,000 francs per annum in 1795.

~ 4 ~

A la citoyenne Bonaparte chez la citoyenne Beauharnais,
Rue Chantereine no. 6, Paris.
Albenga, April 5th.
It is an hour after midnight. They have just brought me a letter. It is a sad one, my mind is distressed – it is the death of Chauvet. He was *commissionaire ordinateur en chef* of the army; you have sometimes seen him at the house of Barras. My love, I need consolation. It is by writing to you, to you alone, the thought of whom can so influence my moral being, to whom I must pour out my troubles. What does the future mean? What does the past mean? What are we? What magic fluid surrounds and hides from us the things that we most need to know? We are born, we live, we die in the midst of marvels; is it surprising that priests, astrologers, charlatans have profited by this fact, by this strange circumstance, to exploit our ideas, and twist them to their own advantage?

Chauvet is dead. He was attached to me. He has rendered essential service to the nation. His last words were that he was setting off to join me. Yes, I see his ghost; it hovers everywhere, it whistles in the air. His soul is in the clouds, he will add luck to my destiny. But, fool that I am, I shed tears for our friendship, and who shall tell me that I should not mourn what can't be changed. Soul of my life, write to me by every courier, or else I shall not know how to exist. I am very busy here. Beaulieu is moving his army again. We are face to face. I am rather tired; I am every day on horseback. Adieu, adieu, adieu; I am going to dream of you. Sleep consoles me; it places you by my side, I clasp you in my arms. But on waking, alas! I find myself three hundred leagues from you. Remembrances to Barras, Tallien, and his wife.

N. B.

Chauvet is dead. – *Chauvet is first mentioned in Napoleon's correspondence in a letter to his brother Joseph, August 9, 1795. Mdme. Junot tells us that Bonaparte was very fond of him, and that he was a man of gentle manners and very ordinary conversation. On March 27th Bonaparte had written to Chauvet from Nice that every day that he delayed joining him, 'takes away from my operations one chance of probability for their success'.*

~5~

A la citoyenne Bonaparte, rue Chantereine no. 6,
Chaussée d'Antin, Paris (address not in B.'s writing.)
Albenga, April 7th.
I have received the letter which you break off in order, you say, to go into the country; and in spite of that you give me to understand that you are jealous of me, here, overwhelmed with business and fatigue. Ah, my dear, it is true I am wrong. In the spring the country is beautiful, and then the lover of nineteen will doubtless find means

to spare an extra moment to write to him who, distant three hundred leagues from you, lives, enjoys, exists only in thoughts of you, who reads your letters as one devours, after six hours' hunting, the meat he likes best.

I am not satisfied with your last letter; it is as cold as friendship. I have not found that fire which kindles your looks, and which I have sometimes fancied I found there. But how infatuated I am. I found that your previous letters weigh too heavily on my mind. The revolution which they produced there invaded my rest, and took my faculties captive. I desired more frigid letters, but they gave me the chill of death. Not to be loved by Josephine, the thought of finding her unfaithful. But I am creating troubles for myself – there are so many real ones, there is no need to make up more!

I have received the letter from Madame Château Renard and I have written to the minister. I will write to the former tomorrow, to whom you will make the usual compliments. Kind regards to Madame Tallien and Barras.

You do not speak of your wretched indigestion – I hate it. Adieu, till tomorrow, *mio dolce amor*. A thought from my unique wife, and a victory from destiny – these are my wishes: a unique remembrance entirely worthy of him who thinks of you every moment.

My brother is here; he has learnt of my marriage with pleasure. He longs to see you. I am trying to prevail on him to go to Paris – his wife has just given birth to a girl. He sends you a gift of a box of Genoa bonbons. You will receive oranges, perfumes, and orange-flower water, which I am sending.

Junot and Murat present their respects to you.

St. Amand notes that Bonaparte begins to suspect his wife in this letter, while the previous ones, especially that of April 3rd, show perfect confidence. Napoleon is on the eve of a serious battle, and has only just put his forces into readiness. On the previous day (April 6th) he wrote to the Directory that the movement against Genoa, of which he does not approve, has brought the enemy out of their winter quarters almost before he has had time to prepare: 'The army is in a state of alarming destitution; I still have great difficulties to overcome, but they are surmountable: misery has excused want of discipline, and without discipline we'll never have a victory. I hope to have all in good shape shortly – there are signs already; in a few days we shall be fighting. The Sardinian army consists of 50,000 foot, and 5,000 horse; I have only 45,000 men at my disposal, all told. Chauvet, the commissary-general, died at Genoa: it is a heavy loss to the army, he was active and enterprising.'

Two days later Napoleon, still at Albenga, reports that he has found Royalist traitors in the army, and complains that the Treasury had not sent the promised pay for the men, 'but in spite of everything, we shall advance'. General Massena, eleven years older than his new commander-in-chief, had received him coldly, but soon became his right-hand man, always genial, and full of good ideas. Massena's men are ill with too much salt meat, they have hardly any shoes, but, as in 1800, he has never a doubt that Bonaparte will make a good campaign, and determines to loyally support him. Another subordinate, Laharpe, so soon to die, is a man of a different stamp – one of those, doubtless, of whom Bonaparte thinks when he writes to Josephine, 'Men trouble me'.

The lover of nineteen. – *The allusion is lost.*

~ 6 ~

A la citoyenne Bonaparte, etc.

Carru, April 24th.

To My Sweet Love,

My brother will bring you this letter. I have for him the most lively affection. I trust he will obtain yours; he merits it. Nature has endowed him with a gentle, even, and unalterably good disposition; he is made up of good qualities. I am writing to Barras to help secure for him the consulate of some Italian port. He wishes to live with his little wife far from the great whirlwind, and from great events. I recommend him to you. I have received your letters of (April) the fifth and tenth. You have not written to me for several days. What *are* you doing then? Yes, my kind, kind love, I am not jealous, but sometimes uneasy. Come soon. I warn you, if you delay you will find me ill; fatigue and your absence are too much for me at the same time.

Your letters make up my daily pleasure, but I don't have many happy days. Junot is bringing twenty-two flags to Paris. You ought to return with him, do you understand? Be ready, if that is not disagreeable to you. Should he not come, woe without remedy; should he come back to me alone, grief without consolation, constant anxiety. My beloved, he will see you, he will breathe on your temples; perhaps you will accord him the unique and priceless favour of kissing your cheek, and I, I shall be alone and very far away; but you are about to come, are you not? You will soon be beside me, on my breast, in my arms. Take wings, come quickly, but travel gently. The route is long, bad, fatiguing. If you should be overturned or be taken ill, if fatigue – go gently, my beloved.

I have received a letter from Hortense. She is entirely lovable. I am going to write to her. I love her much, and I will soon send her the perfumes that she wants.

N. B.

I don't know if you want money, for you never speak to me of business. If you do, will you ask my brother for it – he has 200 louis of mine! If you want to find a position for anyone you can send him; I will give him one. Château Renard may come too.

My brother. – *ie. Joseph. He and Junot reached Paris in five days, and had a great welcome. Carnot, at a dinner-party, showed Napoleon's portrait next to his heart, because 'I foresee he will be the saviour of France, and I wish him to know that he has at the Directory only admirers and friends'.*

If you want to find a position for anyone, you can send him here. I will give him one. – *Bonaparte was beginning to feel firm in the saddle, whilst at Paris Josephine was treated like a princess. On April 25th, Letourneur, as one of the Directory, writes to him, 'A vast career opens itself before you; the Directory has measured the whole extent of it'. In a further letter, bearing the same date, Letourneur insists on a full and accurate account of the battles being sent, as they will be necessary 'for the history of the triumphs of the Republic'. In a private letter to the Directory, dated Carru, April 24th, Bonaparte tells them that when he returns to camp, worn-out, he has to work all night to put matters straight, and repress pillage: 'Soldiers without bread work themselves into an excess of frenzy which makes one blush to be a man.'... 'I intend to make terrible examples. I shall restore order, or cease to command these brigands. The campaign is not yet decided. The enemy is desperate, numerous, and fights well. He knows I am in want of everything, and trusts entirely to time; but I trust entirely to the good genius of the Republic, to the bravery of the soldiers, to the harmony of the officers, and even to the confidence they repose in me.'*

~ 7 ~

To la citoyenne Bonaparte, etc.

To Josephine.

Tortona, noon, June 15.

My life is a perpetual nightmare. Sad thoughts oppress me. I see you no longer. I have lost more than life, more than happiness, more than my rest. I am almost without hope. I hasten to send a courier to you. He will stay only four hours in Paris, and then bring me your reply. Write me ten pages. That alone can console me a little. You are ill, you love me, I have made you unhappy, you are in delicate health, and I do not see you! – that thought destroys me. I have done you so much wrong that I know not how to atone for it; I accuse you of staying in Paris, and you were ill there. Forgive me, my dear; the love with which you have inspired me has bereft me of reason. I shall never find it again. It is an ill for which there is no cure. My presentiments are so ominous that I would confine myself to merely seeing you, to pressing you for two hours to my heart – and then dying with you. Who looks after you? I expect you have sent for Hortense. I love that sweet child a thousand times more when I think she can console you a little, though for me there is neither consolation nor repose nor hope until the courier that I have sent comes back and until, in a long letter, you explain to me what is the nature of your illness, and to what extent it is serious. If it is dangerous, I warn you, I head at once for Paris. My coming shall coincide with your illness. I have always been fortunate, never has my destiny resisted my will, and today I am pained by something which concerns me alone. Josephine, how can you remain so long without writing to me; your last laconic letter is dated May 22nd. Moreover, it is a distressing one for me, but I always keep it in my pocket; your portrait and letters are perpetually before my eyes.

I am nothing without you. I scarcely imagine how I existed without knowing you. Ah! Josephine, had you known my heart would you have waited from May 8th to June 4th before setting off? Would you have given an ear to perfidious friends who perhaps desire to keep you away from me? I openly confess it to every one, I hate everybody who is near you. I expected you to set out on May 24th, and arrive on June 3rd.

Josephine, if you love me, if you realise how everything depends on your health, take care of yourself. I dare not tell you not to undertake so long a journey, and that, too, in the hot weather. At least, if you are fit to make it, come by short stages; write to me at every sleeping-place, and send your letters on ahead.

All my thoughts are concentrated in your boudoir, in your bed, on your heart. Your illness! – that is what occupies me night and day. Without appetite, without sleep, without care for my friends, for glory, for my country, you, you alone – the rest of the world exists no more for me than if it were annihilated. I prize honour since you prize it, I prize victory since it pleases you; without that I should leave everything in order to fling myself at your feet.

Sometimes I tell myself that I worry myself unnecessarily; that even now she is better, that she is leaving, has left, is perhaps already at Lyons. Vain hope! You are in bed suffering, more beautiful, more interesting, more lovable. You are pale and your eyes are more languishing, but when will you be cured? If one of us ought to be ill it is I – more robust, more courageous; I should support illness more easily. Destiny is cruel, it strikes at me through you.

What consoles me sometimes is to think that it is in the power of destiny to make you ill; but it is in the power of no one to make me survive you.

In your letter, dear, be sure to tell me that you are convinced that I love you more than it is possible to imagine; that you are persuaded that all my moments are dedicated to you; that to think of any other woman has never entered my head – they are all in my eyes without grace, wit, or beauty; that you, you alone, such as I see you, such as you are, can please me, and absorb all the faculties of my mind; that you have traversed its whole extent; that my heart has no recess into which you have not seen, no thoughts which are not subordinate to yours; that my strength, my prowess, my spirit are all yours; that my soul is in your body; and that the day on which you change or cease to live will be the day I die; that nature, that earth, is beautiful only because you live. If you do not believe all this, if your soul is not convinced, penetrated by it, you grieve me, you do not love me – there is a magnetic fluid between people who love one another – you know perfectly well that I could not tolerate a rival, much less suffer one. To tear out his heart and to see him would be for me one and the same thing, and then if I were to use my hands against your sacred person – no, I should never dare to do it; but I would quit a life in which the most virtuous of women had deceived me.

But I am sure and proud of your love; misfortunes are the trials which reveal to each of us the whole force of our passion. A child as charming as its mother will soon see the daylight, and will pass many years in your arms. Hapless me! I would be happy with one *day*. A thousand kisses on your eyes, your lips, your tongue, your c***. Most charming of your sex, what is your power over me? I am very sick of your sickness; I have still a burning fever! Do not keep the courier more than six hours, and let him return at once to bring me the longed-for letter of my Beloved.

Do you remember my dream, in which I was your boots, your dress, and in which I made you come bodily into my heart? Why has not nature arranged matters in this way; she has much to do yet.

N. B.

June 15. – *Here occurs the first gap in the correspondence. On April 28th the Armistice of Cherasco was signed, by which Bonaparte's rear was secured by three strong fortresses. He writes to the Directory that Piedmont is at their mercy. He looks upon northern Italy as conquered, and speaks of invading Bavaria through the Tyrol. 'My columns are marching; Beaulieu flees. I hope to catch him. I shall impose a contribution of some millions on the Duke of Parma: he will sue for peace: don't be in a hurry, so that I may have time to make him also contribute to the cost of the campaign, by replenishing our stores and rehorsing our waggons at his expense.' Bonaparte suggests that Genoa should pay fifteen millions in indemnity for the frigates and vessels taken in the port. Certain risks had to be run in invading Lombardy, owing to want of horse artillery, but at Cherasco he secured artillery and horses. Writing to Carnot he states he is marching against Beaulieu, who has 26,000 foot out of 38,000 at commencement of campaign. Napoleon's force is 28,000, but he has less cavalry. On May 1st, in a letter dated Acqui to Citizen Faipoult, he asks for particulars of the pictures, statues, etc., of Milan, Parma, Placentia, Modena, and Bologna. On May 9th Napoleon writes to Carnot,*

'We have at last crossed the Po. The second campaign is begun; Beaulieu... has fool-hardiness but no genius. One more victory, and Italy is ours.' He sends to Paris twenty old masters, with fine examples of Correggio and Michaelangelo. In a letter to Carnot Napoleon writes, 'I owe you my special thanks for the care that you have kindly given to my wife; I recommend her to you, she is a sincere patriot, and I love her to distraction.' He is sending 'a dozen millions' to France, and hopes that some of it will be useful to the army of the Rhine. Nevertheless, his plan of ending the war by an advance through the Tyrol strikes them as too risky. He is to conquer the Milanais, and then divide his army with Kellermann, who is to guard the conquered province, while he goes south to Naples and Rome.

Bonaparte writes directly to Citizen Carnot from Lodi, as well as to the Executive Directory: 'On the receipt of the Directory's letter of the 7th your wishes were fulfilled, and the Milanais is ours. I shall shortly march, to carry out your intentions, on Leghorn and Rome; all that will soon be done. I am writing to the Directory regarding their idea of dividing the army. I swear that I have no thought beyond the interest of my country ... Kellermann will command the army as well as I, for no one is more convinced than I am that the victories are due to the courage and pluck of the army; but I think combining Kellermann and myself in Italy is to lose everything. I cannot serve willingly with a man who considers himself the first general in Europe; and, besides, I believe one bad general is better than two good ones. War is like government: it is an affair of tact. To be of any use, I must enjoy the same confidence that you testified to me in Paris. Where I make war, here or there, is a matter of indifference. To serve my country, to deserve from posterity a page in our history, to give the Government proofs of my attachment and devotion – that is the sum of my ambition. But I am very anxious not to lose in a week the fatigues, anxieties, and dangers of two months, and to find myself fettered. I began with a certain amount of fame; I wish to continue worthy of you.' To the Directory he writes that the expeditions to Leghorn, Rome, and Naples are small affairs, but to be safely conducted must have one general in command. 'I have made the campaign without consulting a soul; I should have done no good if I had had to share my views with another. I have gained some advantages over superior forces,

General Bonaparte entering an enthusiastic Milan through the Romana gate in May 1796

and in utter want of everything, because, certain of your confidence, my marches have been as quick as my thoughts.' He foretells disaster if he is shackled with another general. 'Every one has his own method of making war. General Kellermann has more experience, and will do it better than I; but both together will do it very badly.' With Barras he knew eloquence was useless, and therefore bribed him with a million francs. On May 10th the terrible battle of the Bridge of Lodi was won and where he told Las Cases that he 'was struck with the possibility of becoming famous. It was then that the first spark of my ambition was kindled'.

On May 15th, thirty-five days after the commencement of the campaign, he entered Milan, under a triumphal arch and amid the acclamations of the populace. On May 22nd he returned to Lodi, but heard immediately that Lombardy in general, and Pavia in particular, was in open revolt. He makes a terrible example of Pavia, shooting its chief citizens, and, for the only time, giving up a town to three hours' pillage. The Directory congratulates him on these severe measures: 'The laws of war and the safety of the army render them legitimate in such circumstances'. He writes to them that had the blood of a single Frenchman been spilt, he would have erected a column on the ruins of

Pavia, on which should have been inscribed, 'Here was the town of Pavia'.

On May 21st, Carnot replies to the letter from Lodi: 'You appear desirous, citizen general, of continuing to conduct the whole series of military operations in Italy, at the actual seat of war. The Directory has carefully considered your proposition, and the confidence that they place in your talents and republican zeal has decided this question in the affirmative... The rest of the military operations towards the Austrian frontier and round Mantua are absolutely dependent on your success against Beaulieu. The Directory feels how difficult it would be to direct them from Paris. It leaves to you in this respect the greatest latitude, while recommending the most extreme prudence. Its intention is, however, that the army shall cross into the Tyrol only after the expedition to the south of Italy.'

On May 31st Carnot writes to urge him to press the siege of Mantua, reasserting that the reinforcements which Beaulieu has received will not take from that army its sense of inferiority, and that ten battalions of Hoche's army are on the way. It approves and confirms the 'generous fraternity' with which Bonaparte offers a million francs to the armies on the Rhine.

My life is a perpetual nightmare. – *Napoleon had written to Barras on June 11th declaring that 'I hate all women!'.*

~ 8 ~

To la citoyenne Bonaparte, etc.

To Josephine.

Pistoia, Tuscany, June 26th.

For a month I have only received from my dear love two letters of three lines each. Is she so busy, that writing to her dear love is not necessary, nor, consequently, thinking about him? To live without thinking of Josephine would be death and annihilation to your husband. Your image improves my moods, and enlivens the black and sombre picture of melancholy and grief. A day perhaps may come in which I shall see you, for I doubt not you will be still at Paris, and on that day I will show you my pockets stuffed with letters that I have not sent you because they are too silly (*bête*). Yes, that's the word. Good heavens! Tell me, you who know so well how to make others love you without being in love yourself, do you know how to cure me of love? I will pay a high price for such medicine.

You ought to have set off on May 24th. Being good-natured, I waited till June 1st, as if a pretty woman would give up her habits, her friends, both Madame Tallien and a dinner with Barras, and the acting of a new play, and Fortuné; yes, Fortuné, whom you love much more than your husband, for whom you have only a little of the esteem, and a share of that benevolence with which your heart abounds. Every day I count up your misdeeds. I work myself into a fury in order not to love you any more than I do. Bah, but I do – in fact, my peerless little mother, I will tell you my secret. Defy me, stay at Paris, have lovers – let everybody know it – never write me a monosyllable! Then I shall love you ten times more for it; and it is not folly, a delirious fever! And I shall not get over it. Oh! Would to heaven I could get better! But don't tell me you are ill, don't try to justify yourself. Good heavens! You are pardoned. I love you to distraction, and never will my poor heart cease to give all for love. If you did not love me, my fate would be indeed grotesque. You have not written to me; you are ill, you do not come. But you have passed Lyons; you will be at Turin on the 28th, at Milan on the 30th, where you will wait for me. You will be in Italy, and I shall still be far from you. Adieu, my well-beloved; a kiss on your mouth, another on your heart.

We have made peace with Rome – who gives us money. Tomorrow we shall be at Leghorn, and as soon as I can I'll be in your arms, at your feet, on your bosom.

Between June 15th and the renewal of Josephine's correspondence a glance at the intervening dates will show that Bonaparte and his army were not wasting time. The treaty with Rome was a masterpiece as, in addition to money and works of art,

Mme Tallien.

Pope Pius VI.

he obtained the port of Ancona, siege-guns with which to bombard Mantua, and, best of all, a letter from the Pope to the faithful of France, recommending submission to the new government there. It was not, however, until February 1797 that the Pope fulfilled his obligations under this Treaty, and then under new compulsion.

Madame Tallien. – *Théresia Cabarrus was the principal attraction of Barras' circle. She was Josephine's closest friend in 1795.*

Fortuné. – *Josephine's dog (see note to Letter 10).*

You ought to have set off. – *Josephine actually left Paris on June 27th. She was accompanied by Hippolyte Charles, a dashing young cavalry officer. Charles, whose real name was Louis-Hippolyte Quentin, was 24 in 1796. Their dalliance continued into 1798, Josephine writing to him on March 17th 1798 that 'they all hate me, you, tender you, are my true love. I shall kill myself. I shall end a life which is empty if it can not be devoted to you. What have I done to these monsters?'. Joseph Bonaparte was also part of the group as was Junot who, reportedly, spent the nights with Josephine's maid, Louise Compoint, whilst Josephine slept with Charles.*

~ 9 ~

To Josephine, at Milan.
Roverbella, July 6, 1796.
I have beaten the enemy. Kilmaine will send you the copy of the despatch. I am tired to death. Pray start at once for Verona. I need you, for I think that I am going to be very ill.

I send you a thousand kisses. I am in bed.

Bonaparte

In one of his several letters to the Directory on this date we can see Bonaparte's anxiety for reinforcements; the enemy has already 67,000 men against his 40,000. Meanwhile he is helping the Corsicans to throw off the British yoke, and believes that the French possession of Leghorn will enable them to gain that island without firing a shot.

~ 10 ~

To Josephine, at Milan.
Marmirolo, July 17, 1796, 9 p.m.
I got your letter, my beloved; it has filled my heart with joy. I am grateful to you for the trouble you have taken to send me news; your health should be better today – I am sure you have recovered. Get out and ride a horse, which cannot fail to do you good.

Ever since I left you, I have been sad. My happiness is to be by your side. I never stop thinking about your kisses, your tears, your enchanting jealousy; and the charms of the incomparable Josephine keep constantly alight a bright and burning flame in my heart and my being. When will it be that, free from every worry, from all business, I can spend all my moments at your side, to have nothing to do but to love you, and to prove it to you? I shall send your horse, but I am hoping that you will soon be able to rejoin me. I thought I loved you some days ago; but, since I saw you, I feel that I love you even a thousand times more. Ever since I have known you, I worship you more every day; which proves how false is the maxim of La Bruyère that 'Love is sudden'. Everything in nature has a regular course, and different degrees of growth. Ah! Show me some of your faults; be less beautiful, less gracious, less tender, and, especially, less kind; above all never be jealous, never weep; your tears madden me, fire my blood. Be sure that it is no longer possible for me to have a thought except for you, or an idea of which doesn't serve you.

Have a good rest. Get well soon. Come and join me, so that, at least, before dying, we could say – 'We were happy for so many days!!'

Millions of kisses, and even to Fortuné, in spite of his naughtiness.

Bonaparte

Marmirolo. – *On July 12th he writes to the Directory from Verona that for some days he and the enemy have been watching each other. 'Woe to the one who makes a false move'. He indicates that he is about to make a* coup de main *on Mantua with 300 men dressed in Austrian uniforms. He is by no means certain of success, which 'depends entirely on luck – either on a dog or a goose'. He complains of much sickness among his men round Mantua, owing to the heat and stench from the marshes, but so far no deaths. He will be ready to make Venice disgorge a few millions shortly, if the Directory make a quarrel in the interim.*

Josephine had arrived in Milan on July 9th. On the 13th he was with Josephine, as he writes from Milan but leaves on the 14th. Napoleon frequently kissed and fondled his wife in public; Antoine-Romain Hamelin, witness to such passion, was embarrassed by this public display 'and always went to look out of the window to see what the weather was like'.

Fortuné. – *Arnault tells an anecdote of this dog, which in 1794, in the days of the Terror, had been used as a bearer of secret despatches between Josephine in prison and the governess of her children outside the grille. Henceforward Josephine would never be parted from it. One day in June 1797 the dog was lying on the same couch as its mistress, and Bonaparte, accosting Arnault and pointing to the dog with his finger, said, 'You see that dog there. He is my rival.*

He was in possession of Madame's bed when I married her. I wished to make him get out – vain hope! I was told I must resign myself to sleep elsewhere, or consent to share with him. That was sufficiently exasperating, but it was a question of taking or leaving, and I resigned myself. The favourite was less accommodating than I. I bear the proof of it on this leg.'

Not content with barking at every one, he not only bit men but other dogs, and was finally killed by a mastiff, much to Bonaparte's secret satisfaction; for, as St. Amand adds, 'he could easily win battles, accomplish miracles, make or unmake principalities, but could not show a dog the door.'

~ 11 ~

To Josephine, at Milan.

Marmirolo, July 18, 1796, 2 p.m.

I passed the whole night under arms. I ought to have had Mantua by a bold and fortunate coup; but the waters of the lake have suddenly fallen, so that the column I had despatched could not land. This evening I shall try again, but I'm not sure if the results will be satisfactory.

I got a letter from Eugène, which I send you. Please write from me to these charming children of yours, and send them some presents. Be sure to tell them that I love them as if they were my own. What is yours or mine is so mixed up in my heart, that there is no difference there.

I am very anxious to know how you are, what you are doing? I have been in the village of Virgil, on the banks of the lake, by the silvery light of the moon, and not a moment without dreaming of Josephine.

The enemy tried a big sortie on June 16th; it has killed or wounded two hundred of our men, but they lost five hundred in a hasty retreat.

I am well. I am Josephine's entirely, and I have no pleasure or happiness except in her company.

Three Neapolitan regiments have arrived at Brescia; they have separated themselves from the Austrian army, in consequence of the convention I have concluded with M. Pignatelli.

I've lost my snuff-box; please choose me a flat one, and write something pretty inside, and include some of your own hair.

A thousand kisses as burning as you are cold.

Limitless love, and utter fidelity. Before Joseph leaves, I wish to speak to him.

Bonaparte

~ 12 ~

To Josephine, at Milan.

Marmirolo, July 19, 1796.

I have been without letters from you for two days. That is at least the thirtieth time today that I have made this observation to myself; you think that's sad; yet you cannot doubt the tender and unique anxiety with which you inspire me.

We attacked Mantua yesterday. We warmed it up from two batteries with red-hot shot and from mortars. All night long that miserable town has been on fire. The sight was horrible and imposing. We have secured several of the outworks; we start digging trenches tonight. Tomorrow I leave for Castiglione with the staff, and I reckon on sleeping there. I have received a courier from Paris. There were two letters for you; I have read them. But though this action appears to me quite natural, and though you gave me permission to do so the other day, I fear you may be cross, and that is a great trouble to me. I should have liked to have sealed them up again: that would have been atrocious. If I am to blame, I beg your forgiveness. I swear that it is not because I am jealous; assuredly not. I have too high an opinion of my beloved for that. I should like you to give me permission to read your letters, then there would be no longer either remorse or apprehension.

Achille has just ridden post from Milan; no letters from my beloved! Adieu, my unique joy. When will you be able to rejoin me? I shall have to fetch you myself from Milan.

A thousand kisses as fiery as my heart, as pure as you.

I have summoned the courier; he tells me that he crossed over to your house, and that you told him you had no commands. Naughty, ugly, cruel, tyrannous, pretty little monster. You laugh at my threats, at my silliness; ah, you know only too well that if I could lock you up in my breast, I would put you in prison there!

Tell me you are cheerful, in good health, and very affectionate.

Bonaparte

Achille. – *Murat. He had been appointed one of Bonaparte's aides-de-camp; February 29th, made General of Brigade after the Battle of Lodi (May 10th); is sent to Paris after Junot with nine trophies, and arrives there first. He flirts there outrageously with Josephine, but does not escort her back to her husband.*

~ 13 ~

To Josephine, at Milan.

Castiglione, July 21, 1796, 8 a.m.

I had hoped that I would have found one of your letters when I arrived here. You know, my dear Josephine, the pleasure they give me; and I am sure you have pleasure in writing them. I am leaving tonight for Peschiera, for the mountains of – –, for Verona, and from there I shall go to Mantua, and perhaps to Milan, to receive a kiss, since you assure me they are not cold there. I hope you will be perfectly well by then, and will be able to accompany me to headquarters, so that we may not part again. Are you not the soul of my life, and the all the sentiments of my heart?

Your protégés are a little excitable. How glad I can do something for them which will please you. They will go to Milan. A little patience is requisite in everything.

Adieu, *belle et bonne*, quite unequalled, quite divine. A thousand loving kisses.

Bonaparte

~ 14 ~

To Josephine, at Milan.

Castiglione, July 22, 1796.

The needs of the army require my presence here; it is impossible that I can leave it to come to Milan. In five or six days something might happen which might make my presence here essential.

You assure me your health is good; I beg you therefore to come to Brescia. Even now I am sending Murat to prepare quarters for you in the town, as you desire.

I think you will do well to spend the first night (July 24th) at Cassano, setting out very late from Milan; and to arrive at Brescia on July 25th, where the most affectionate of lovers awaits you. I am disconsolate that you can believe, dear, that my heart can reveal itself to others as well as to you; it belongs to you by right of conquest, and that conquest will be durable and for ever. I do not know why you speak of Madame T., with whom I do not concern myself in the slightest, nor with the women of Brescia. As to the letters which you are cross at my opening, it won't happen again; your letter had not come.

Adieu, *ma tendre amie*, send me news often, come at once and join me, and be happy and at ease; all goes well, and my heart is yours for life.

Be sure to return to the Adjutant-General Miollis the box of medals that he tells me he has sent you. Men have such false tongues, and are so wicked, that it is necessary to have everything just so.

Good health, love, and a prompt arrival at Brescia.

I have at Milan a carriage suitable alike for town or country; you can make use of it for the journey. Bring your china with you, and some of the things you absolutely require.

Travel by easy stages, and when it is cool, so as not to tire yourself. Troops only take three days coming to Brescia. Travelling post it is only a fourteen-hour journey. I request you to sleep on the 24th at Cassano; I shall come to meet you on the 25th at latest.

Adieu, my own Josephine. A thousand loving kisses.

Bonaparte

The needs of the army. – *Difficulties were accumulating, and Napoleon was, as he admits at St. Helena, seriously alarmed. Wurmser's force proves to be large, Piedmont is angry with the Republic and ready to rise, and Venice and Rome would willingly follow its example; the English have taken Porto Ferrajo, and their skilful minister, Windham, is sowing the seeds of discord at Naples. Although on July 20th Bonaparte has written to a friend in Corsica that 'all smiles on the Republic', he tells Saliceti, another Corsican, another story on August 1st: 'Fortune appears to oppose us at present. ... I have raised the siege of Mantua; I am at Brescia with nearly all my army. I shall take the first opportunity of fighting a battle with the enemy which will decide the fate of Italy – if I'm beaten, I shall retire on the Adda; if I win, I shall not stop in the marshes of Mantua. ... Let the citadels of Milan, Tortona, Alessandria, and Pavia be provisioned. ... We are all very tired; I have ridden five horses to death.' Reading between the lines of this letter to Josephine, it is evident that he thinks she will be safer with him than at Milan – Wurmser having the option of advancing via Brescia on Milan, and cutting the French communications. The Marshal's fatal mistake was in using only half his army for the purpose. This raising of the siege of Mantua (July 31st) was heart-rending work for Bonaparte, but he had no artillery horses, and it was better to lose the siege train than to jeopardise the whole army. Wurmser had begun his campaign successfully by defeating Massena, and pushing back Sauret at Salo. Bonaparte had been perfectly honest in telling the Directory his difficulties, and sends his brother Louis to the Directory for that purpose on the eve of battle. He is complimented in a letter from the Directory dated August 12th – a letter probably the more genuine as they had just received a further despatch announcing a victory. On August 3rd Bonaparte won a battle at Lonato, and the next day Augereau gained great laurels at Castiglione. Between July 29th and August 2nd the French army took 15,000 prisoners, 70 guns, and wounded or killed 25,000, with little more than half the forces available to the Austrians. Bonaparte gives his losses at 7,000, exclusive of the 15,000 sick he has in hospital. From July 31st to August 6th he never changed his boots, or lay down in a bed.*

A thousand loving kisses. – *Napoleon's passion is reflected in one of Josephine's letters to Madame Tallien. On July 23rd she writes: 'My husband does not love me; he worships me. I think he'll go mad. It is impossible to be happier than I am at his side'. She then tells Tallien about Barras and that 'I love him a lot and my heart is devoted to him'.*

~ 15 ~

To Josephine, at Milan.

Brescia, August 30, 1796.

Arriving, my beloved, my first thought is to write to you. Your health, your sweet face and body have not been absent a moment from my thoughts the whole day. I shall be comfortable only when I have got letters from you. I await them impatiently. You cannot possibly imagine my uneasiness. I left you cross, annoyed, and unwell. If the deepest and sincerest affection can make you happy, you ought to be. I am worked to death.

Adieu, my kind Josephine: love me, keep well, and often, often think of me.

Bonaparte

Brescia. – *Napoleon was here on July 27th, meeting Josephine about the date arranged (July 25th), and she returned with him. On July 29th Josephine was nearly captured by an Austrian ambush near Ceronione, and Josephine wept with fright. 'Wurmser', said Napoleon, embracing her, 'shall pay dearly for those tears'. She accompanies him to Castel Nova, and sees a skirmish at Verona; but the sight of wounded men makes her leave the army, and, finding it impossible to reach Brescia, she flees via Ferrara and Bologna to Lucca. Thence she goes via Florence to Milan. The Austrian army was broken and in full retreat, and Bonaparte conducts his correspondence from Brescia from August 11th to 18th. On August 13th Bonaparte sent to the Directory his opinion of most of his generals, in order to show that he required some better ones. Some of his criticisms are interesting:*

Berthier – 'Talents, activity, courage, character; he has them all.'

Augereau – 'Much character, courage, firmness, activity; is accustomed to war, beloved by the soldiers, lucky in his operations.'

Massena – 'Active, indefatigable, has boldness, grasp, and promptitude in making his decisions.'

Serrurier – 'Fights like a soldier, takes no responsibility; determined, has not much opinion of his troops, is often sick.'

Despinois – 'Flabby, inactive, slack, has not the genius for war, is not liked by the soldiers, does not fight with his head; has nevertheless good, sound political principles: would do well to command in the interior.'

Sauret – 'A good, very good soldier, not sufficiently enlightened to be a general; unlucky.'

On the 25th he is at Milan, where he meets his wife after her long pilgrimage, and spends four days. By August 30th he is again at Brescia, and reminds her that he left her 'cross, annoyed, and not well'.

~ 16 ~

To Josephine, at Milan.

Brescia, August 31, 1796.

I'm leaving at once for Verona. I had hoped to get a letter from you; and I am terribly worried about you. You were rather ill when I left; I beg you not to leave me in such uncertainty. You promised me to be more regular; and, at the time, your tongue was in harmony with your heart. You, to whom nature has given a kind, genial, and wholly charming disposition, how can you forget the man who loves you with so much fervour? No letters from you for three days; and yet I have written to you several times. To be parted is dreadful, the nights are long, stupid, and wearisome; the day's work is monotonous.

This evening, alone with my thoughts, work and correspondence, with men and their stupid schemes, I have not even one letter from you which I might press to my heart.

The staff has gone; I set off in an hour. Tonight I get a despatch from Paris; there was for you only the enclosed letter, which will please you.

Think of me, live for me, be often with your loved one, and be sure that there is only one misfortune that he is afraid of – that of being no longer loved by his Josephine. A thousand kisses, very sweet, very affectionate, very much for you alone. Send M. Monclas at once to Verona; I will find him a place. He must get there before September 4th.

Bonaparte

From a letter to her aunt, Madame de Renaudin, at this time, quoted by Aubenas, we can see Josephine's real feelings: 'I am fêted wherever I go; all the princes of Italy give me parties, even the Grand Duke of Tuscany, brother of the Emperor. Ah, well, I prefer being a private individual in France. I care not for honours bestowed in this country. I get sadly bored. My health has undoubtedly a great deal to do with making me unhappy; I am often out of sorts. If happiness could assure health, I ought to be in the best of health. I have the most amiable husband imaginable. I have no time to long for anything. My wishes are his. He is all day long in adoration before me, as if I were a divinity; there could not possibly be a better husband. M. Serbelloni will tell you how he loves me. He often writes to my children; he loves them dearly. He is sending Hortense, by M. Serbelloni, a lovely repeater, jewelled and enamelled; to Eugène a splendid gold watch.'

~ 17 ~

To Josephine, at Milan.

Alla, September 3, 1796.

The campaign has well and truly begun, my love; we have driven in the enemy's outposts; we have taken eight or ten of their horses and a similar number of cavalrymen. My troops are happy and in excellent spirits. I hope that we shall do great things, and get into Trent by the fifth.

No letters from you, which really makes me uneasy; yet they tell me you are well, and have even had an excursion to lake Como. Every day I wait impatiently for the post which will bring me news of you – you are well aware how I prize it. Far from you I cannot live, the happiness of my life is near my gentle Josephine. Think of me! Write to me often, very often: in absence it is the only remedy: it is cruel, but, I hope, will only be temporary.

I hope that we shall do great things, and get into Trent by the fifth. – *He entered the city on that day. In his pursuit of Wurmser, he and his army cover sixty miles in two days, through the terrific Val Saguna and Brenta gorges, brushing aside opposition on the way.*

~ 18 ~

To Josephine, at Milan.
Montebello, noon, September 10, 1796.
My Dear,
The enemy has lost 18,000 men prisoners; the rest killed or wounded. Wurmser, with a column of 500 cavalry, and 500 infantry, had no alternative but to throw himself into Mantua.

Never have we had successes so unvarying and so great. Italy, Friuli, the Tyrol, are assured to the republic. The Emperor will have to create a second army: artillery, pontoons, baggage, everything is taken.

In a few days we shall meet; it is the sweetest reward for my labours and anxieties.

A thousand fervent and very affectionate kisses,

Bonaparte

~ 19 ~

To Josephine, at Milan.
Ronco, September 12, 1796, 10 a.m.
My dear Josephine,
I have been here two days, badly lodged, badly fed, and very cross at being so far from you.

Wurmser is trapped, he has with him 3,000 cavalry and 5,000 infantry. He is at Porto-Legnago; he is trying to get back into Mantua, but for him that has now become impossible. The moment this matter shall be finished I will be in your arms.

I embrace you a million times.

Bonaparte

~ 20 ~

To Josephine, at Milan.
Verona, September 17, 1796.
My Dear,
I write very often and you seldom. You are naughty, and ugly; very ugly, as well as thoughtless. It is disloyal to deceive a poor husband, an affectionate lover. Should he lose his rights just because he is far away, up to his neck in duty, worries and anxiety. Without his Josephine, without the assurance of her love, what in the wide world remains for him. What will he do?

Yesterday we had a very bloody fight; the enemy has lost heavily, and been completely beaten. We have taken from him the suburbs of Mantua.

Adieu, charming Josephine; one of these nights the door will burst open with a bang, I'll be like a jealous husband, and, soon, in your arms.

A thousand loving kisses.

Bonaparte

One of these nights the doors will burst open with a bang. – *Apparently within two or three days, for Bonaparte is at Milan on September 21st, and stays with his wife till October 12th.*

On October 1st he writes to the Directory that his total forces are only 27,900; and that the Austrians, within six weeks, will have 50,000. He asks for 26,000 more men to end the war satisfactorily: 'If the preservation of Italy is dear to you, citizen directors, send me help'. On the 8th they reply with the promise of 10,000 to 12,000, to which he replies (October 11th) that if 10,000 have started only 5,000 will reach him. The Directory at this time are poverty stricken, and ask him once more to pay Kellermann's Army of the Alps, as being 'to some extent part of that which you command'. This must have been odd for the general who was to have been superseded by Kellermann just a few months previously. For some time these letters had been signed by the President Lareveillere Lepeaux, but on September 19th there was a charming letter from Carnot: 'Although accustomed to unprecedented deeds on your part, our hopes have been surpassed by the victory of Bassano. What glory is yours, immortal Bonaparte! Moreau was about to effect a juncture with you when that wretched coward *Jourdan upset all our plans. Do not forget that immediately the armies go into winter quarters on the Rhine the Austrians will have forces available to help Wurmser.' At Milan Bonaparte advises the Directory that he is dealing with unpunished 'fripponeries' in the commissariat department. Here he receives from young Kellermann, afterwards the hero of Marengo, a* report *of the condition of the Brescia fever-hospitals, dated October 6th: 'A wretched mattress, dirty and full of vermin, a coarse sheet to each bed, rarely washed, no counterpanes, much dilatoriness, such is the spectacle that the fever hospitals of Brescia present; it is heart-rending. The soldiers justly complain that, having conquered opulent Italy at the cost of their life-blood, they might, without enjoying comforts, at least find the help and attention which their situation demands. Bread and rice are the only passable foods, but the meat is hard. I beg that the general-in-chief will immediately give attention to his companions in glory, who wish for restored health only that they may gather fresh laurels.'*

On October 12th he tells the Directory that Mantua will not fall till February. On the same day he shows them that all the marvels of his six months' campaign have cost the French Government only £440,000 (eleven million francs). He pleads, however, for special auditors to have charge of the accounts. Napoleon had not only made war support war, but had sent twenty million francs requisitioned in Italy to the Republic. On October 12th he leaves Milan for Modena, where he remains from the 14th to the 18th, is at Bologna on the 19th, and Ferrara from the 19th to the 22nd, reaching Verona on the 24th.

By this time Bonaparte is heartily sick of the war. On October 2nd he writes direct to the Emperor of Germany: 'Europe wants peace. This disastrous war has lasted too long'; and on the 16th to Marshal Wurmser: 'The siege of Mantua, sir, is more disastrous than two campaigns.' His weariness is tempered with policy, as the Austrian Alvinzi was en route, and the French reinforcements had not arrived, not even the 10,000 promised in May.

~ 21 ~

To Josephine, at Milan.

Modena, October 17, 1796, 9 p.m.

The day before yesterday I was out the whole day. Yesterday I stayed in bed. Fever and a violent headache prevented me writing to my beloved; but I got your letters. I have pressed them to my heart and lips, and the grief of a hundred miles of separation has disappeared. I can see you by my side, not capricious and cross, but gentle, affectionate, with that kindness unique to my Josephine. It was a dream, judge if it has cured my fever. Your letters are as cold as if you were fifty; we might have been married fifteen years. That's how you write in the winter of life. Oh, Josephine. It is very naughty, very unkind, very unfaithful of you. What more can you do to make me an object for compassion? Love me no longer? Eh, that is already accomplished! Hate me? Well, I'd prefer that as everything's stale except hate; indifference, is worse with its marble pulse, its rigid stare, its monotonous demeanour!

A thousand thousand very heartfelt kisses.

I am rather better. I'm leaving tomorrow. The English evacuate the Mediterranean. Corsica is ours. Good news for France, and for the army.

Bonaparte

Corsica is ours. – *At St. Helena he told his generals, 'The King of England wore the Corsican crown only two years. This whim cost the British treasury five millions sterling. John Bull's riches could not have been worse employed'. He writes to the Directory that: 'The expulsion of the English from the Mediterranean has considerable influence on the success of our military operations in Italy. We can exact more onerous conditions from Naples, which will have the greatest moral effect on the minds of the Italians, assures our communications, and makes Naples tremble as far as Sicily.' On October 25th he writes: 'Wurmser is at his last gasp; he is short of wine, meat, and forage; he is eating his horses, and has 15,000 sick. In fifty days Mantua will either be taken or delivered.'*

~ 22 ~

To Josephine, at Milan.

Verona, November 9, 1796.

My Dear,

I have been at Verona since the day before yesterday. Although tired, I am very well, very busy; and I love you passionately at all times. I am just off on horseback.

I embrace you a thousand times.

Bonaparte

Verona. – *Bonaparte had made a long stay at Verona, to November 4th, awaiting reinforcements which never came. On November 5th he writes to the Directory: 'Fine promises and a few driblets of men are all we have received' and on November 13th he writes again: 'Perhaps we are on the brink of losing Italy. None of the expected reinforcements have arrived. ... I am doing my duty, the officers and men are doing theirs; my heart is breaking, but my conscience is at rest. Help – send me help !... I despair of preventing the relief of Mantua, which in a week would have been ours. The wounded are the pick of the army; all our superior officers, all our picked generals are* hors de combat; *those who have come to me are so incompetent, and they do not have the soldiers' confidence. The army of Italy, reduced to a handful of men, is exhausted. The heroes of Lodi, Millesimo, Castiglione, and Bassano have died for their country, or are in hospital; to the corps remain only their reputation and their glory. Joubert, Lannes, Lanusse, Victor, Murat, Chabot, Dupuy, Rampon, Pijon, Menard, Chabran, and St. Hilaire are wounded. ... In a few days we shall make one last effort. Had I received the 83rd, 3,500 strong, and of good reputation in the army, I would have answered for everything. Perhaps in a few days 40,000 will not suffice.' The reason for such unwonted pessimism was the state of his troops. His brother Louis reported that Vaubois' men had no shoes and were almost naked, in the midst of snow and mountains; that desertions were taking place of soldiers with bare and bleeding feet, who told the enemy the plans and conditions of their army. Finally Vaubois bungles, through not knowing the ground, and is put under the orders of Massena, while two of his demi-brigades are severely censured by Napoleon in person for their cowardice.*

Verona, November 9th, noon.

My Adored Josephine,

Once more I breathe freely. Death is no longer before me, and glory and honour are once more re-established. The enemy is beaten at Arcola. Tomorrow we will repair Vaubois' blunder of abandoning Rivoli. In a week Mantua will be ours, and then your husband will clasp you in his arms, and give you a thousand proofs of his ardent affection. I shall proceed to Milan as soon as I can; I am rather tired. I have received letters from Eugène and Hortense – charming young people. I will send them to you as soon as I find my belongings, which are at present somewhat dispersed.

We have made five thousand prisoners, and killed at least six thousand of the enemy. Goodbye, my adored Josephine. Think of me often. If you cease to love your Achilles, if for him your heart grows cold, you will be very cruel, very unjust. But I am sure you will always remain my faithful mistress, as I shall ever remain your fond lover. Death alone can break the chain which sympathy, love, and sentiment have forged. Let me have news of your health A thousand and a thousand kisses.

From Bourrienne s Life of Napoleon, *vol. i. Chap. 4.*

Once more breathe freely. – *Napoleon had been foiled, as much by the weather and his shoeless soldiers as by numbers (40,000 Austrians to his 28,000), and his position was well-nigh hopeless on November 14th. He trusts Verona to 3,000 men, and the blockade of Mantua to Kilmaine, and the defence of Rivoli to Vaubois – the weakest link in the chain – and determines to manoeuvre against the Austrian communications. He gets forty-eight hours' start, and wins Arcola. The battle of Arcola lasted seventy-two hours, and for forty-eight hours was in favour of the Austrians. Pending the arrival of the promised reinforcements, the battle cost the French heavily. Napoleon replaced Vaubois by Joubert.*

~ 24 ~

To Josephine, at Milan.

Verona, November 23, 1796.

I don't love you a bit; on the contrary, I detest you. You are common, clumsy, silly and don't have a thought in your head. You never write to me; you don't care for your husband; you know the pleasure your letters give him, and you write him barely half-a-dozen lines scribbled down at random.

How, then, do you spend the day, madam? What business of such importance robs you of the time to write to your very kind lover? What inclination stifles and alienates love, the affectionate and unvarying love which you promised me? Who can this brilliant man be, this new lover who takes up all your time, is master of your days, and prevents you from thinking about your husband? Josephine, be on your guard; one fine night the doors will be broken in, and I shall be before you.

Really, my dear, I am worried that there's no news from you. Write me four pages immediately, and some of those charming remarks which fill my heart with feelings and pleasure.

I hope that before long I shall clasp you in my arms, and cover you with a million kisses as hot as if they were from the equator.

Bonaparte

~ 25 ~

Verona, November 24, 1796.

I hope soon, darling, to be in your arms. I love you to distraction. I am writing to Paris by this courier. All goes well. Wurmser was beaten yesterday under Mantua. Your husband only needs Josephine's love to be happy.

Bonaparte

~ 26 ~

To Josephine, at Genoa.

Milan, November 27, 1796, 3 p.m.

I get to Milan; I fling myself into your room; I have left all in order to see you, to clasp you in my arms. You were not there. You senselessly gad about the towns; you run further from me when I get close; you care no longer for your dear Napoleon. A passing fancy made you love him; fickleness renders him indifferent to you.

Used to perils, I know the remedy for weariness and the ills of life. The ill-luck that I now suffer is past all calculations; I did right not to anticipate it.

I shall be here till the evening of the 29th. Don't alter your plans;

have your pleasure; happiness was invented for you. The whole world is only too happy if it can please you, and only your husband is very, very unhappy.

Bonaparte

Evening of the 29th. – *But he stays at Milan from November 27th to December 16th. The picture by Gros of Bonaparte, flag in hand, leading his men across the murderous bridge of Arcola features on the jacket of this book and it was during this visit to Milan that he sat for his portrait. Lavalette has preserved for us the domestic rather than the dignified manner of the sitting. Napoleon refused to give a fixed time, and the artist was in despair, until Josephine came to his aid by taking her husband on her knees every morning after breakfast, and keeping him there a short time. Lavalette assisted at three of these sittings. From December 16th to 21st Bonaparte is at Verona, from where he returns to Milan. There is perhaps a veiled innuendo in Barras' letter of December 30th. Clarke had advised the Directory that the Austrian General Alvinzi was planning an attack, which Barras mentions, but adds: 'Your return to Milan shows that you consider another attack in favour of Wurmser unlikely, or, at least, not imminent.' He is at Milan till January 7th, from where he goes to Bologna, the city which, he says, 'of all the Italian cities has constantly shown the greatest energy and the most considerable share of real information'.*

~ 27 ~

To Josephine, at Genoa.
Milan, November 28, 1796, 8 p.m.
I have received the courier whom Berthier had hurried on to Genoa. You have not had time to write me, I feel it intuitively. Surrounded with pleasures and pastimes, you would be wrong to make the least sacrifice for me. Berthier has been good enough to show me the letter which you wrote to him. My intention is that you should not

make the least change in your plans, nor with respect to the pleasure parties in your honour. I am of no consequence, either the happiness or the misery of a man whom you don't love is a matter of no importance.

For my part, to love you only, to make you happy, to do nothing which may anger you, that is the object and goal of my life.

Be happy, do not reproach me, do not concern yourself in the happiness of a man who lives only in your life, rejoices only in your pleasure and happiness. When I exacted from you a love like my own I was wrong; why expect lace to weigh as heavily as gold? When I sacrifice to you all my desires, all my thoughts, every moment of my life, I obey the sway which your charms, your disposition, and your whole personality have so effectively exerted over my unfortunate heart. I was wrong, since nature has not given me attractions with which to captivate you; but what I do deserve from Josephine is her regard and esteem, for I love her frantically and uniquely.

Farewell, beloved wife; farewell, my Josephine. May fate concentrate in my breast all the grief and troubles, but may it give Josephine happy and prosperous days. Who deserves them more? When it shall be quite settled that she can love me no more, I will hide my profound grief, and will content myself with the power of being useful and serviceable to her.

I reopen my letter to give you a kiss. Ah! Josephine! ... Josephine!

Bonaparte

~ 28 ~

To Josephine, at Milan.
Verona, January 12, 1797.
I had hardly left Roverbella when I learnt that the enemy had appeared at Verona. Massena made some dispositions, which have been very successful. We have made six hundred prisoners, and have

taken three cannon. General Brune got seven bullets in his clothes, without being hit by one of them – this is what it is to be lucky.

I give you a thousand kisses. I am very well. We have had only ten men killed, and a hundred wounded.

Bonaparte

General Brune. – *On January 12, 1797, he also wrote to General Clarke from Verona (No. 1375 of the* Correspondence*) almost an exact duplicate of this letter – a very rare coincidence in the epistles of Napoleon. 'Scarcely set out from Roverbella, I learnt that the enemy had appeared at Verona. Massena made his dispositions, which have been very successful; we have made 600 prisoners, and we have taken three cannon. General Brune has had seven bullets in his clothes, without having been touched by one of them; this is what it is to be lucky. We have had only ten men killed, and a hundred wounded.' Bonaparte had left Bologna on January 10, reaching Verona via Roverbella on the 12th.*

~ 29 ~

To Josephine, at Bologna.
Forli, February 3, 1797.
I wrote to you this morning. I'm leaving tonight. Our forces are at Rimini. This country is beginning to be tranquillised. My cold makes me always rather tired.

I idolise you, and send you a thousand kisses.

A thousand kind messages to my sister.

Bonaparte

I wrote to you this morning. – *This and probably other letters describing Rivoli, La Favorite, and the imminent fall of Mantua, are missing. In summing up the campaign Thiers declares that in ten months 55,000 French (all told, including reinforcements) had beaten more than 200,000 Austrians, taken 80,000 of them prisoners, killed and wounded 20,000. They had fought twelve pitched battles, and sixty actions. These figures are probably as much above the mark as those of Napoleon's detractors are below it.*

~ 30 ~

To Josephine, at Bologna.
Ancona, February 10, 1797.
We have been at Ancona these two days. We took the citadel, after a slight fusillade, and by a *coup de main*. We made 1,200 prisoners. I sent the fifty officers to their homes.

I am still at Ancona. I do not insist you come, because everything is not yet settled, but in a few days I am hoping that it will be. Besides, this country is still discontented, and everybody is nervous.

I start tomorrow for the mountains. You don't write to me at all, yet you ought to let me have news of you every day.

Please go out every day; it will do you good.

I send you a million kisses. I never was so sick of anything as of this vile war.

Goodbye, my darling. Think of me!

Bonaparte

~ 31 ~

To Josephine, at Bologna.
Ancona, February 13, 1797.
I get no news from you, and I feel sure that you no longer love me. I have sent you the papers, and various letters. I start immediately to cross the mountains. The moment that I know something definite, I will arrange for you to accompany me; it is the dearest wish of my heart.

A thousand and a thousand kisses.

Bonaparte

~ 32 ~

To Josephine, at Bologna.

February 16, 1797.

You are sad, you are ill; you no longer write to me, you want to go back to Paris. Do you no longer love your friend? The thought makes me unhappy. My darling, life is unbearable for me now that I am aware of your sadness.

I make haste to send you Moscati, so that he may look after you. My health is rather bad; I still have my cold. Please take care of yourself, love me as much as I love you, and write to me every day. I am more worried than ever.

I have told Moscati to escort you to Ancona, if you care to come there. I will write to you there, to let you know where I am.

Perhaps I shall make peace with the Pope, then I shall soon be by your side; it is my soul's most ardent wish.

I send you a hundred kisses. Be sure that nothing equals my love, unless it be my worry. Write to me every day yourself. Goodbye, dearest.

Bonaparte

Moscati. – *Francesco Moscati, a young Italian officer of Neapolitan extraction who died in London in 1847.*

Perhaps I shall make peace with the Pope. – *On February 12th the Pope had written to 'his dear son, General Bonaparte', to appoint plenipotentiaries for a peace, and ends by assuring him 'of our highest esteem', and concluding with the paternal apostolic benediction. Meanwhile Napoleon, instead of sacking Faenza, has just invoked the monks and priests to follow the precepts of the Gospel.*

~ 33 ~

To Josephine, at Bologna.

Tolentino, February 19, 1797.

Peace with Rome has just been signed. Bologna, Ferrara, Romagna, are ceded to the Republic. The Pope is to soon pay us thirty millions, as well as works of art.

I am leaving tomorrow morning for Ancona, and then for Rimini, Ravenna, and Bologna. If your health permits, come to Rimini or Ravenna, but, I beg you, take care of yourself.

Not a word from you – Good God! What have I done? I think of nothing but you, I love only Josephine, I live only for my wife, I enjoy happiness only with my dear one – does this deserve such harsh treatment from her? My dear, I beg you, think often of me, and write to me every day.

You are either ill or you do not love me! Do you think, then, that I have a heart of stone? And do my sufferings concern you so little? You don't know me! I cannot believe it! You to whom nature has given intelligence, tenderness, and beauty, you who alone can rule my heart, you who doubtless know only too well the unlimited power you hold over me!

Write to me, think of me, and love me.

Yours for life.

Bonaparte

The unlimited power you hold over me. – *There seems no question that during the Italian campaigns he was absolutely faithful to Josephine, although there was scarcely a beauty in Milan who did not want to please him or to have him. In his fidelity there was, says St. Amand, much love and a little calculation. As Napoleon has said himself, his position was delicate in the extreme; he commanded old generals; every one of his movements was jealously watched; his circumspection was extreme. The celebrated singer, La Grassini, who had all Italy at her feet, was besotted with the young general who scarcely paid her any attention.*

The Consul

Napoleon, one of three Consuls, rules France after his return from Egypt. Napoleon is in the centre with Cambacérès on the left and Lebrun on the right.

After victory in Italy Napoleon, as ambitious as ever, set off for Egypt with an expeditionary force. Initially successful, the French ran into difficulties in Syria and had their fleet destroyed by Nelson. Meanwhile, back in Europe, the situation went from bad to worse. On August 23rd, 1799, Napoleon quits Egypt and sails for France. He is in Paris by October 13th. Then, on November 9th, he dissolved the Directory and, the following day, dismisses the Council of the Five Hundred. It is an audacious coup. That December he is proclaimed First Consul.

His relationship with Josephine had been almost as eventful. Josephine had been guilty of some indiscretion whilst Napoleon was in Egypt and his return to Paris was marked by a sequence of quarrels which almost caused a permanent rift between the two. War, as so frequently before, again intervened and in early 1800, Napoleon left Paris for another campaign against the Austrians in Italy.

~ 1 ~

To Josephine, at Paris.

Lausanne, May 15, 1800.

I have been at Lausanne since yesterday. I'm leaving tomorrow. My health is fairly good. The country around here is very beautiful. I see no reason why, in ten or twelve days, you should not join me here; you must travel incognito, and not say where you are going, because I want no one to know what I am about to do. You can say you are going to Plombières.

I will send you Moustache, who has just arrived.

My very kindest regards to Hortense. Eugène will not be here for eight days; he is on his way.

Elected to the joint consulate by the events of the 18th Brumaire *(November 9th), 1799, Napoleon spent the first Christmas Day after his return from Egypt in writing personal letters to the King of England and Emperor of Austria, with a view to peace. He asks King George how it is that the two most enlightened nations of Europe do not realise that peace is the chief need as well as the chief glory ... and concludes by asserting that the fate of all civilised nations is bound up in the conclusion of a war 'which embraces the entire world'. His efforts fail in both cases. On December 27th he makes the* Moniteur *the only official newspaper. On April 22nd he urges Moreau to begin his campaign with the army of the Rhine, an order reiterated on April 24th through Carnot, again made Minister of War. A diversion to save Massena's army of Italy was now imperative. On May 5th he congratulated Moreau on the battle of Stockach, but informs him that Massena's position is critical, trapped in Genoa, and with food only till May 25th. He advises Massena the same day that he leaves Paris that night to join the Army of Reserve, that the 'cherished child of victory' must hold out as long as possible, at least until May 30th.*

Moustache. – *Napoleon's personal courier, Colonel Claustres from the Ariège.*

~ 2 ~

To Josephine, at Paris.

Torre di Garofolo, May 16, 1800.

I am leaving immediately to spend the night at Saint-Maurice. I have not received a single letter from you; that is no good. I have written you by every courier.

Eugène may arrive the day after tomorrow. I have a bit of a cold, but it will have no ill effects.

My very kindest regards to you, my good little Josephine, and to all who belong to you.

Bonaparte

~ 3 ~

To Madame Bonaparte

(address not in Bonaparte's writing.)

Ivrea, May 29th, 1800, 11 p.m.

I hardly know which way to turn. In an hour I start for Vercelli. Murat

Napoleon painted by Appiani in 1802 with an olive branch to mark the Peace of Amiens.

Josephine luxuriates at the now stylish Malmaison in 1800.

ought to be at Novara tonight. The enemy is thoroughly demoralised; he cannot even yet understand us. I hope within ten days to be in the arms of my Josephine, who is always very good when she is not crying and not flirting. Your son arrived this evening. I have had him examined; he is in excellent health. Accept a thousand tender thoughts. I have received M.'s letter. I will send her by the next courier a box of excellent cherries.

We are here – within two months for Paris.

Yours entirely,

N. B.

This letter is from Tennant's Tour, etc., *Vol. ii.*

On the 30th Napoleon is at Vercelli, on June 1st at Novara, and on June 2nd in Milan. Eugène served under Murat at the passage of the Ticino, May 31st.

M.'s – *probably 'Maman', his mother.*

~ 4 ~

To Josephine, at Paris.

Milan.

I am at Milan, with a very bad cold. I can't stand rain, and I have been wet to the skin for several hours, but all goes well. I won't persuade you to come here. I shall be home in a month.

I trust to find you flourishing. I am just leaving for Pavia and Stradella. We are masters of Brescia, Cremona, and Placentia.

Kindest regards.

Murat has borne himself splendidly.

Milan. – *He arrived here on June 2nd, and met with a great reception. In his bulletin of June 5th we find him assisting at an improvised concert. It ends, somewhat quaintly for a bulletin, as follows: 'Italian music has a charm ever new. The celebrated singers, Billington, La Grassini, and Marchesi are expected at Milan. They say they are about to start for Paris to give concerts there.' According to M. Frédéric Masson, this Paris visit masked ulterior motives, and was arranged at breakfast on the same day, where La Grassini, Napoleon, and Berthier ate together. Grassini was in Paris in July, causing Josephine to exclaim to Madame Krény on July 9th 'I am so unhappy, my dear, Bonaparte is causing such rows and I don't know why. This isn't what life should be. I tried to find the cause of all this and learnt that Grassini has been in Paris for eight days. She seems to be the cause of all the pain I am suffering'.*

To Josephine, at Plombières.

Paris the '27'.., 1801.

The weather is so bad here that I have remained in Paris. Malmaison, without you, is too dreary. The fête has been a great success; it has rather tired me. The blister they have put on my arm gives me constant pain.

Malmaison was purchased by Josephine in April 1799 for 225,000 francs.

Some plants have come for you from London, which I have sent to your gardener. If the weather is as bad at Plombières as it is here, you will suffer severely from floods.

Best love to 'Maman' and Hortense.

Bonaparte

The date is doubtless 27 Messidor *(July 16), and the fête alluded to that of July 14th. The next day Napoleon signed the Concordat with the Pope, which paved the way for the restoration of Roman Catholicism in France (September 11th).*

The blister. – *On July 7th he quaintly writes to Talleyrand: 'They have put a second blister on my arm, which prevented me giving audience yesterday. Time of sickness is an opportune moment for coming to terms with the priests.'*

Some plants. – *No trait in Josephine's character is more characteristic than her love of flowers. The splendid hothouses of Malmaison, constructed by M. Thibaut, had been modelled on those of Kew, and enabled Josephine to collect exotics from every climate, and especially from her beloved Martinique. The Minister of Marine instructed captains to bring back floral examples from the tropics and these sometimes fell, together with the ships, into the hands of the British. The Prince Regent usually had them sent on from London. Her curator, M. Aimé Bonpland, was an accomplished naturalist, who had been with Humboldt in America, and brought back 6,000 new plants. On his return in 1804 he was nominated by Josephine manager of the gardens of Malmaison and Navarre.*

Malmaison, without you, is too dreary. – *Although Madame La Grassini had been specially summoned to sing at the Fête de la Concorde the day before.*

~ 6 ~

To Josephine, at Plombières.

Malmaison, June 19, 1802.

I have as yet received no news from you, but I think you must already have begun to take the waters. It is rather dull for us here, although your charming daughter does the honours of the house to perfection. For the last two days I have suffered slightly from my complaint. The fat Eugène arrived yesterday evening; he is very hale and hearty.

I love you as I did the first hour, because you are kind and sweet beyond compare.

Hortense told me that she was often writing to you.

Best wishes, and a love-kiss.

Yours ever, Bonaparte

This is the third pilgrimage Josephine has made, under the doctor's orders, to Plombières; but the longed-for heir will have to be sought for elsewhere, by fair means or foul. Lucien, who as Ambassador to Spain, had vainly spent the previous year in arranging the divorce and remarriage of Napoleon to a daughter of the King of Spain, suggests adultery at Plombières, or a 'warming-pan conspiracy', as the last alternatives. Josephine complains to Napoleon of his brother's 'poisonous' suggestions, and Lucien is again disgraced. In a few months an heir is found in Hortense's first-born, Napoleon Charles, born October 10th.

The fat Eugène. – *Josephine's son had come partly to be near his sister in her mother's absence, and partly to receive his colonelcy. Josephine is upset, and writes to Hortense (June 16th): 'I am utterly wretched, my dear Hortense, to be separated from you, and my mind is as sick as my body. I feel that I was not born, my dear child, for so much grandeur. ... By now Eugène should be with you; that thought consoles me.' Aubenas has found in the Tascher archives a charming letter from Josephine to her mother in Martinique, announcing how soon she may hope to find herself a great-grandmother.*

~ 7 ~

To Josephine, at Plombières.

Malmaison, June 23, 1802.

My good little Josephine,

Your letter has come. I am sorry to see you have been poorly on the journey, but a few days' rest will put you right. I am very fairly well. Yesterday I was at the Marly hunt, and one of my fingers was very slightly injured whilst shooting a boar.

Hortense is usually in good health Your fat son has been rather unwell, but is getting better. I think the ladies are playing 'The Barber of Seville' tonight. The weather is perfect.

Rest assured that my truest wishes are ever for my little Josephine.

Yours ever, Bonaparte

Your letter has come. – *Possibly the one to Hortense quoted above, as Josephine was not fond of writing many letters.*

Injured whilst shooting a boar. – *The account in the* Memorial of St. Helena *is as follows: – 'Another time, while hunting the wild boar at Marly, all his suite were put to flight; it was like the rout of an army. The Emperor, with Soult and Berthier, maintained their ground against three enormous boars. "We killed all three, but I received a hurt from my adversary, and nearly lost this finger", said the Emperor, pointing to the third finger of his left hand, which indeed bore the mark of a severe wound. "But the most laughable circumstance of all was to see the multitude of men, surrounded by their dogs, screening themselves behind the three heroes, and calling out lustily 'Save the Emperor! Save the Emperor!' while not one advanced to my assistance"'(vol. ii. 202. Colburn, 1836). 'Save the Emperor' is an anachronism; he was at the time First Consul.*

The Barber of Seville. – *This was their best play, and spectators (except Lucien) agree that in it the little theatre at Malmaison and its actors were unsurpassed in Paris. Bourrienne as Bartholo and Hortense as Rosina excelled. According to the Duchesse d'Abrantes, Wednesday was the usual day of representation, when the First Consul was wont to ask forty persons to dinner, and a hundred and fifty for the evening. As the Duchess had reason to know, Bonaparte was the severest of critics. 'Lauriston made a noble lover', says the Duchess – 'rather heavy' being Bourrienne's comment. Eugène, says Méneval, excelled in footman's parts. Michot, from the Theatre Francais, was stage manager; and Bonaparte provided their costumes and a collection of dramas. Lucien, who refused to act, declares that Bonaparte quoted the saying of Louis XVI concerning Marie Antoinette and her company, that the performances 'were royally badly played'.*

~ 8 ~

To Josephine, at Plombières.

Malmaison, June 27, 1802.

Your letter, dear little wife, has apprised me that you are out of sorts. Corvisart tells me that it is a good sign that the baths are having the desired effect, and that your health will soon be re-established. But I am most truly grieved to know that you are in pain.

Yesterday I went to see the Sèvres factory at St. Cloud.

Best wishes to all.

Yours for life, Bonaparte

The Sèvres factory. – *After his visit, he wrote to Duroc: 'This morning I gave, in the form of gratuity, a week's wages to the workmen of the Sèvres factory. Have the amount given to the director. It should not exceed a thousand* écus.*'*

~ 9 ~

To Josephine, at Plombières.

Malmaison, July 1, 1802.

Your letter of June 28th has arrived. You say nothing of your health nor of the effect of the spa. I see that you expect to be home in a week; that is good news for your lover, who is tired of being alone!

You ought to have seen General Ney, who started for Plombières; he will be married on his return.

Yesterday Hortense played Rosina in 'The Barber of Seville' with her usual skill. Rest assured of my love, and that I await your return impatiently. Without you everything here is dreary.

Bonaparte

Your lover, who is tired of being alone. – *So much so that he got up at five o'clock in the morning to read his letters in a young bride's bed-chamber. The story is brightly told by the lady in question, Madame d'Abrantes (vol. ii. ch. 19). A few days before the Marly hunt, mentioned above, the young wife of seventeen, whom Bonaparte had known from infancy, and whose mother (Madame Permon) he had hoped to marry, found the First Consul seated by her bedside with a thick packet of letters, which he was carefully opening and making marginal notes upon. At six he went off singing, pinching the lady's foot through the bed-clothes as he went. The next day the same thing happened, and the third day she locked herself in, and prevented her maid from finding the key. In vain – the unwelcome visitor fetched a master-key. As a last resource, she persuaded her husband, General Junot, into breaking orders and spending the night with her; and the next day (June 22nd) Bonaparte came in and found his old comrade of Toulon, fast asleep, by her side. The latter dreamily but good-humouredly asked,*

'Why, General, what are you doing in a lady's chamber at this hour?' and the former replied, ' I came to awake Madame Junot for the hunt, but I find her provided with an alarm still earlier than myself. I could tell you off, for you are not supposed to be here, M. Junot.' He then withdrew, after offering Junot a horse for the hunt. The husband jumped up, exclaiming, 'Faith! that is an amiable man! What goodness! Instead of scolding, instead of sending me sneaking back to my duty in Paris! Confess, my Laura, that he is not only an admirable being, but above the sphere of human nature.' Laura, however, was still dubious. Later in the day she was taken to task by the First Consul, who was astounded when she told him that his action might compromise her. 'I shall never forget', she says, 'Napoleon's expression of countenance at this moment; it displayed a rapid succession of emotions, none of them evil.' Josephine heard of the episode, and was jealous for some little time to come.

General Ney. – *Bonaparte had instructed Josephine to find him a nice wife, and she had chosen Mlle. Agläe-Louise Auguié, the intimate friend and schoolfellow of Hortense, and daughter of a former Receveur-Général des Finances. Napoleon (who stood godfather to all the children of his generals) and Hortense were sponsors for the firstborn of this union, Napoleon Joseph, born May 8th, 1803. The Duchess d'Abrantes describes her first meeting with Madame Ney at the Boulogne fête of August 15th, 1802. Her simplicity and timidity 'were the more attractive inasmuch as they formed a contrast to most of the ladies by whom she was surrounded at the court of France. ... The softness and benevolence of Madame Ney's smile, together with the intelligent expression of her large dark eyes, rendered her a very beautiful woman, and her lively manners and accomplishments enhanced her personal graces' (vol. iii. 31). The brave way in which she bore her husband's execution won the admiration of Napoleon, who at St. Helena coupled her with Mdme. de Lavalette and Mdme. Labedoyère.*

The Emperor

Napoleon crowned himelf Emperor in December 1804. Here he is amongst his newly-created Marshals of the Empire.

Success and ambition went hand-in-hand and enabled Napoleon to contemplate a further advancement in prestige and power. On May 18th 1804 the First Consul was declared Emperor of France, Josephine his Empress. A plebiscite confirmed this act, 3,500,000 voting in favour of the step, 2,000 resisting it. On December 2nd, despite having invited the Pope to Paris, Napoleon crowned himself. Four months later he declared himself King of Italy.

France was disappointed if it thought that empire meant peace and Napoleon was soon waging war against Austria and Russia (in 1805), Prussia (in 1806), Russia (in 1807 and 1812) and Spain and Portugal (1807-1814). England, as ever, lurked behind every Continental alliance and ringed France with the power of the Royal Navy.

For Napoleon, more and more, dynastic ambition came to the fore. He promoted his family and sought an heir. Josephine did not produce one, try as she might. Imperial tensions began to play on the imperial couple.

~ 1 ~

To the Empress Josephine.

Pont-de-Bricques, July 21, 1804.

Madame and dear Wife,

During the four days that I have been away from you I have always been either on horseback or in a conveyance, without any ill effect on my health.

M. Maret tells me that you intend starting on Monday; travelling by easy stages, you can take your time and reach the spa without tiring yourself.

The wind having considerably freshened last night, one of our gunboats, which was in the harbour, broke loose and ran on the rocks about a league from Boulogne. I believed all lost – men and merchandise; but we managed to save both. The spectacle was grand: the shore wreathed in fire from the alarm guns, the sea raging and bellowing, the whole night spent in anxiety to save these unfortunates or to see them perish! My soul hovered between eternity, the ocean, and the night. At 5 a.m. all was calm, everything saved; and I went to bed with the feeling of having had a romantic and epic dream – a circumstance which might have reminded me that I was all alone, had weariness and soaked garments left me any other need but that of sleep.

Napoleon.

Pont-de-Bricques – *a little village about a mile from Boulogne. On his first visit to the latter he was met by a deputation of farmers, of whom one read out the following address: 'General, here we are, twenty farmers, and we offer you a score of big, sturdy lads, who are, and always shall be, at your service. Take them along with you, General; they will help you to give England a good thrashing. As for ourselves, we have another duty to fulfil: with our arms we will till the ground, so that bread shall not be wanting for the brave fellows who are destined to destroy the English'. Napoleon thanked the honest yeomen, and determined to make the only habitable dwelling there his headquarters. The place is named after the bricks found there – the remains of one of Caesar's camps.*

Madame. – *Napoleon became Emperor on May 18th, and this was the first letter to his wife since Imperial etiquette had become* de rigueur, *and the first letter to Josephine signed Napoleon.*

The wind having considerably freshened. – *Constant tells a good story of the Emperor's obstinacy, but also of his bravery, a few days later. Napoleon had ordered a review of his ships, which Admiral Bruix had ignored, seeing a storm imminent. Napoleon sends off Bruix to Holland in disgrace, and orders the review to take place; but when, amid the wild storm, he sees 'more than twenty gunboats run aground', and no way to save the drowning men, he springs into the nearest lifeboat, crying, 'We must save them somehow'. A wave breaks over the boat; he is drenched and nearly carried overboard, losing the hat he had worn at Marengo. In spite of all that could be done, two hundred lives were lost. This is Constant's version; probably his loss is exaggerated. The Emperor, writing to Talleyrand on August 1st, speaks only of three or four ships lost, and 'a dozen men'.*

~ 2 ~

To the Empress, at Aix-La-Chapelle.

Boulogne, August 3, 1804.

My Dear,

I trust soon to learn that the waters have done you much good. I am sorry to hear of all the worries that have dogged you. Please write to me often. My health is very good, although I am rather tired. I shall be at Dunkirk in a very few days, and shall write to you from there.

Eugène has started for Blois.

I cover you with kisses.

Napoleon

Correspondence of Napoleon I, *No. 7861, communicated by M. Chambry.*

The waters. – *Dr. Corvisart had accompanied the Empress to Aix, to superintend the effect of the sulphurous springs there which was, as usual, nil. Josephine was attempting rudimentary fertility treatment at Aix and Plombières.*

All the worries. – *Constant (vol. i. 230, etc., 1896) is of use to explain what these were having obtained possession of a diary of the tour by one of Josephine's ladies-in-waiting, which had fallen into Napoleon's hands. In the first place, the roads, where there were any (the Emperor had himself planned the itinerary, and had mistaken a projected road for a completed one, between Rethel and Marche), were frightful, especially in the Ardennes forest, and the diary for August 1st concludes by stating 'that some of the carriages were so battered that they had to be bound together with ropes. One ought not to expect women to travel about like a gang of dragoons'. Another concern was the published report of her gift to the Mayoress of Rheims of a malachite medallion set in diamonds, and of her saying as she did so, 'It is the colour of Hope'. Although she had really used this expression, it was the last thing she would like to see in print, taking into consideration the reason for her yearly visits to Plombières, and now to Aix, and their invariable inefficiency. On August 14th the writer of the diary wrote a severe criticism of Josephine: 'She is exactly like a ten-year-old child – good-*

natured, frivolous, impressionable; in tears at one moment, and comforted the next. ... She has just sense enough not to be an utter idiot. Ignorant – as are most Creoles – she has learned nothing, or next to nothing, except by conversation; but, having passed her life in good society, she has got good manners, grace, and a mastery of that sort of jargon which, in society, sometimes passes for wit. Social events constitute the canvas which she embroiders, which she arranges, and which give her a subject for conversation. She is witty for quite a whole quarter of an hour every day. ... Her diffidence is charming ... her temper very sweet and even; it is impossible not to be fond of her. I fear that... this need to confess everything, of communicating all her thoughts and impressions, of telling all that passes between herself and the Emperor, keeps the latter from taking her into his confidence. ... She told me this morning that, during all the years she had spent with him, never once had she seen him let himself go.'

Eugène has started for Blois. – *Where he became the head of the electoral college of Loir et Cher, having just been made Colonel General of the Chasseurs by Napoleon. The Beauharnais family were originally natives of Blois.*

~ 3 ~

To the Empress, at Aix-La-Chapelle.

Calais, August 6, 1804.

My Dear,

I arrived at Calais at midnight; I expect to start tonight for Dunkirk. I am in very fair health, and satisfied with what I see. I trust that the waters are doing you as much good as exercise, camp, and seascape are doing me.

Eugène has set off for Blois. Hortense is well. Louis is at Plombières.

I am longing to see you. You are always necessary to my happiness. My very best love.

Napoleon

The Emperor Napoleon I, painted in imperial robes by Gérard.

The Empress Josephine by Gérard (courtesy of Diana Reid Haig).

~ 4 ~

To the Empress, at Aix-La-Chapelle.

Ostend, August 14, 1804.

My Dear,

I have not had a letter from you for several days; yet I should be more comfortable if I knew that the waters were working, and how you spend your time. During the past week I have been at Ostend. The day after tomorrow I shall be at Boulogne for a somewhat special fête. Advise me by the courier what you intend to do, and how soon you expect to end your baths.

I am very well satisfied with the army and the flotillas. Eugène is still at Blois. I hear no more of Hortense than if she were on the Congo. I am writing to scold her.

My best love to all.

During the past week. – *As a matter of fact he only reached Ostend on April 12th from Boulogne, having left Dunkirk on the 11th.*

The day after tomorrow. – *This fête was the distribution of the Legion of Honour at Boulogne and a review of 80,000 men.*

Hortenses. – *She arrived at Boulogne, with her son, and the Prince and Princess Murat, a few days later, and saw the Emperor. Josephine received a letter from Hortense soon after Napoleon joined her (September 2nd), to which she replied on September 8th. 'The Emperor has read your letter; he has been rather cross not to hear from you occasionally. He would not doubt your kind heart if he knew it as well as I, but appearances are against you. Since he can think you are neglecting him, lose no time in repairing the wrongs which are not real', for 'Bonaparte loves you like his own child, which adds much to my affection for him.'*

I am very well satisfied ... with the flotillas. – *The descent upon England was to have taken place in September, when the death of Admiral Latouche-Tréville at Toulon, August 18th, altered all Napoleon's plans. Around this time Fulton submitted his steamship invention to Bonaparte. The latter, however, had recently been caught out by some useless discoveries, and sends Fulton's plans to the* savants *of the Institute, who report it chimerical and impracticable.*

~ 5 ~

To the Empress, at Aix-La-Chapelle.

Arras, Wednesday, August 29, 1804.

Madame and dear Wife,

I have just reached Arras. I shall stay there tomorrow. I shall be at Mons on Friday, and on Sunday at Aix-la-Chapelle. I am as well satisfied with my journey as with the army. I think I shall pass through Brussels without stopping there; thence I shall go to Maestricht, I am rather impatient to see you. I am glad to hear you have tried the waters; they cannot fail to do you good. My health is excellent. Eugène is well, and is with me.

Very kindest regards to every one.

Bonaparte

Two points are noteworthy in this letter – (1) that it commences Madame and dear Wife; and (2) it is signed Bonaparte and not Napoleon, which might be an old habit.

Arras, August 29th. – *On the 30th he writes Cambacérès from Arras that he is 'satisfied with the spirit of this department'. On the same day he writes to the King of Prussia and Fouché. To his Minister of Police he writes: 'That detestable journal,* Le Citoyen français, *seems only to wish to wallow in blood. For eight days running we have been entertained with nothing but the Saint Bartholomew's Day Massacre. Who on earth is the editor of this paper? With what gusto this wretch relishes the crimes and misfortunes of our fathers! My intention is that you should put a stop to it. Have the owner of this paper changed, or suppress it.' On Friday he is at Mons (writing interesting letters respecting the removal of church ruins), and reaches his wife on the Sunday (September 2nd) as his letter predicted.*

I am rather impatient to see you. – *The past few months had been an anxious time for Josephine. Talleyrand (who thought her his enemy) was scheming for her divorce, and wished Napoleon to marry the Princess of Baden, and thus cement an alliance with Bavaria and Russia. The Bonapartes were very anxious that Josephine should not be crowned. Talleyrand was out of favour, as a diary fell into the emperor's hands in which Talleyrand called him 'a regular little Nero' in his system of espionage.*

Translated from a Letter in the Collection of Baron Heath, Philobiblon Society, vol. xiv.

~ 6 ~

To Josephine, at St. Cloud.

Treves, October 6, 1804.

My Dear,

I arrive at Treves the same moment that you arrive at St. Cloud. I am in good health. Do not grant an audience to T., and refuse to see him. Receive B. only in general company, and do not give him a private interview. Make promises to sign marriage contracts only after I have signed them.

Yours ever, Napoleon

T. – *This may be Talleyrand, whom Mdme. de Rémusat in a letter to her husband (September 21st) at Aix, hinted to be on bad terms with the Emperor, a fact confirmed and explained by Méneval. It may also have been Tallien, who returned to France in 1802, where he had been divorced from his unfaithful wife.*

B. – *Doubtlessly Bourrienne, who was in disgrace with Napoleon, and who was always trying to impose on Josephine's good nature. No sooner had Napoleon left for Boulogne on July 14th than his former secretary inflicts himself on the wife at Malmaison.*

Napoleon joins Josephine at St. Cloud on or before October 13th, where preparations are already being made for the Coronation by the Pope – the first ceremony of the kind for eight centuries.

~ 7 ~

To Josephine, at Strasburg.
Imperial Headquarters Ettlingen,
October 2, 1805, 10 a.m.
I am well, and still here. I am starting for Stuttgart, where I shall be tonight. Great operations are now in progress. The armies of Württemberg and Baden have joined mine. I am well placed for the campaign, and I love you.

Napoleon

Strasburg. – *She is in the former Episcopal Palace, at the foot of the cathedral.*

Stuttgart. – *He has driven over from the Elector of Württemberg's palace at Ludwigsburg on October 4th, and hears the German opera 'Don Juan'.*

I am well placed. – *On the same day Napoleon writes to his brother Joseph*

The coronation of the imperial couple in Notre Dame, Paris, as painted by David.

that he has already won two great victories – (1) by having no sick or deserters, but many new conscripts; and (2) because the Badenese army and those of Bavaria and Württemberg had joined him, and all Germany was well disposed.

~ 8 ~

To Josephine, at Strasburg.
Ludwigsburg, October 4, 1805, noon.
I am at Louisbourg. I'm leaving tonight. There is as yet nothing new. My whole army is on the march. The weather is splendid. My junction with the Bavarians is effected. I am well. I trust in a few days to have something interesting to communicate.

Keep well, and believe in my entire affection. There is a brilliant Court here, a new bride who is very beautiful, and upon the whole some very pleasant people, even our Electress, who appears extremely kind, although the daughter of the King of England.

Napoleon

A new bride. – *This letter, in the collection of his Correspondence ordered by Napoleon III, concludes at this point*

Electress. – *The Princess Charlotte-Auguste-Mathilde (1766-1828), daughter of George III, who married Frederick I of Württemberg. Napoleon says she is 'not well treated by the Elector, to whom, nevertheless, she seems much attached' (Brotonne, No. III). She was equally pleased with Napoleon, and wrote home how astonished she was to find him so polite and agreeable a person.*

~ 9 ~

To Josephine, at Strasburg.

Louisbourg, October 5, 1805.

I continue my march immediately. You will, my dear, be five or six days without hearing from me; don't be uneasy, it is connected with operations now taking place. All goes well, and just as I could wish.

I have assisted at a marriage between the son of the Elector and a niece of the King of Prussia. I wish to give the young princess a wedding present to cost 36,000 to 40,000 francs. Please attend to this, and send it to the bride by one of my chamberlains, when they shall come to rejoin me. This matter must be attended to immediately.

Adieu, dear, I love you and embrace you.

Napoleon

I have assisted at a marriage. – *The bride was the Princess of Saxe-Hildburghhausen, who was marrying the second son of the Elector.*

~ 10 ~

To Josephine, at Strasburg.

Augsburg, Thursday, October 10, 1805, 11 a.m.

I napped at the residence of the former Elector of Trèves, who is very well off. For the past week I have been hurrying forward. The campaign has been successful enough so far. I am very well, although it rains almost every day. Events crowd on us rapidly. I have sent to France 4,000 prisoners, 8 flags, and have 14 of the enemy's cannon.

Adieu, dear, I embrace you.

Napoleon

~ 11 ~

To Josephine, at Strasburg.
October 12, 1805, 11 p.m.
My army has entered Munich. On one side the enemy is beyond the River Inn; I hold the other army, 60,000 strong, blocked on the Iller, between Ulm and Memmingen. The enemy is beaten, has lost its head, and everything points to a most glorious campaign, the shortest and most brilliant which has been made. In an hour I start for Burgau on the Iller.

I am well, but the weather is frightful. It rains so much that I change my clothes twice a day.

I love and embrace you.

Written at Augsburg. On October 15th he reaches the abbey of Elchingen, which is situated on a height, from where a wide view is obtained, and establishes his headquarters there.

~ 12 ~

To Josephine, at Strasburg.
Abbaye d'Elchingen, October 19, 1805.
My dear Josephine,
I have tired myself more than I should have. Soaked garments and cold feet every day for a week have made me rather ill, but I have spent the whole of today indoors, which has rested me.

My plan has been accomplished; I have destroyed the Austrian army by marches alone; I have made 60,000 prisoners, taken 120 cannon, more than 90 flags, and more than 30 generals. I am about to fling myself on the Russians; they are lost men. I am satisfied with my army. I have only lost 1,500 men, of whom two-thirds are but slightly wounded.

Prince Charles is on his way to cover Vienna. I think Massena should be already at Vicenza.

The moment I can give my thoughts to Italy, I will make Eugène win a battle.

Very best wishes to Hortense.

Adieu, my Josephine; kindest regards to every one.

Napoleon

Spent the whole of today indoors. – *This is also mentioned in his Seventh Bulletin (dated the same day), which adds, 'But repose is not compatible with the direction of this immense army.'*

Vicenza. – *Massena did not, however, reach this place till November 3rd. The French editions have Vienna, but Vicenza is evidently meant.*

~ 13 ~

To the Empress, at Strasburg.

Elchingen, October 21, 1805, noon.

I am fairly well, my dear. I leave at once for Augsburg. I have made 33,000 men lay down their arms, I have from 60,000 to 70,000 prisoners, more than 90 flags, and 200 cannon. Never has there been such a catastrophe in military annals!

Take care of yourself. I am rather jaded. The weather has been fine for the last three days. The first column of prisoners heads off for France today. Each column consists of 6,000 men.

Napoleon

He is still at Elchingen, but at Augsburg the next day. On the 21st he issues a decree to his army that Vendémiaire *(the first month of the Republican Calendar), of which this was the last day but one, should be counted as a campaign for pensions and military services.*

Elchingen. – *Méneval speaks of this village 'rising in an amphitheatre above the Danube, surrounded by walled gardens, and houses rising one above the other'. From it Napoleon saw the city of Ulm below, commanded by his cannon. Marshal Ney won his title of Duke of Elchingen by capturing it on October 14th, and fully deserved it. The Emperor used to leave the abbey every morning to go to the camp before Ulm, where he used to spend the day, and sometimes the night.*

Such a catastrophe. – *At Ulm General Mack, with eight fieldmarshals, seven lieutenant-generals, and 33,000 men surrender. Napoleon had despised Mack even in 1800, when he told Bourrienne at Malmaison, 'Mack is a man of the lowest mediocrity I ever saw in my life; he is full of self-sufficiency and conceit, and believes himself equal to anything. He has no talent. I should like to see him some day opposed to one of our good generals; we should then see fine work. He is a boaster, and that is all. He is really one of the most silly men existing, and besides all that, he is unlucky' (vol. i. 304).*

~ 14 ~

To the Empress, at Strasburg.

Augsburg, October 25, 1805.

The two past nights have thoroughly rested me, and I am going to start tomorrow for Munich. I am sending word to M. de Talleyrand and M. Maret to be near at hand. I shall see something of them, and I am going to advance upon the Inn in order to attack Austria in the heart of her hereditary states. I should much have liked to see you; but do not reckon upon my sending for you, unless there should be an armistice or winter quarters.

Adieu, dear; a thousand kisses. Give my compliments to the ladies.

Napoleon

~ 15 ~

To the Empress, at Strasburg.

Munich, Sunday, October 27, 1805.

I received your letter per Lemarois. I was grieved to see how needlessly you have made yourself unhappy. I have heard particulars which have proved how much you love me, but you should have more fortitude and confidence. Besides, I had advised you that I should be six days without writing to you.

Tomorrow I expect the Elector. At noon I start to support my advance on the Inn. My health is fair. You need not think of crossing the Rhine for two or three weeks. You must be cheerful, amuse yourself, and hope that before the end of the month we shall meet.

I am advancing against the Russian army. In a few days I shall have crossed the Inn.

Adieu, my dear; kindest regards to Hortense, Eugène, and the two Napoleons.

Keep back the wedding present a little longer.

Yesterday I gave a concert to the ladies of this court. The choirmaster is a superior man.

I took part in the Elector's pheasant-shoot; you see by that that I am not so tired. M. de Talleyrand has come.

Napoleon

Munich. – *Napoleon arrived here on October 24th.*

Lemarois. – *A trusty aide-de-camp, who had witnessed Napoleon's civil marriage in March 1796, at 10 p.m.*

I was grieved. – *They had no news from October 12th to 21st in Paris, where they learnt daily that Strasburg was in the same predicament. Mdme. de Rémusat, at Paris, was equally anxious, and such women, in the Emperor's absence, tended by their presence or even by their correspondence to increase the alarms of Josephine.*

The end of the month. – *The month* Brumaire, *i.e. before November 21st.*

Talleyrand has come. – *He was urgently needed to help in the correspondence with the King of Prussia (concerning the French violation of his Anspach territory), with whom Napoleon's relations were becoming more strained.*

~ 16 ~

To the Empress, at Strasburg.

Haag, November 3, 1805, 10 p.m.

I am in full march; the weather is very cold, the earth covered with a foot of snow. This is rather trying. Luckily there is no want of wood; here we are always in forests. I am fairly well. My campaign proceeds satisfactorily; my enemies must have more anxieties than I.

I wish to hear from you and to learn that you are not worrying yourself.

Adieu, dear; I am going to lie down.

Napoleon

My enemies. – *Later in the day Napoleon writes from Lambach to the Emperor of Austria a pacific letter, which contains the paragraph, 'My ambition is wholly concentrated on the re-establishment of my commerce and of my navy, and England grievously opposes itself to both.'*

~ 17 ~

To the Empress, at Strasburg.

Tuesday, November 5, 1805.

I am at Lintz. The weather is fine. We are within seventy miles of Vienna. The Russians do not stand; they are in full retreat. The house of Austria is at its wit's end, and in Vienna they are removing all the court belongings. It is probable that something new will occur within five or six days. I much desire to see you again. My health is good.

I embrace you.

Napoleon

~ 18 ~

To the Empress, at Strasburg.
November 15, 1805, 9 p.m.
I have been at Vienna two days, my dear, rather tired. I have not yet seen the city by day; I have traversed it by night.

Tomorrow I receive the notables and public bodies. Nearly all my troops are beyond the Danube, in pursuit of the Russians.

Adieu, Josephine; as soon as it is possible I will send for you. My very best love.

Napoleon was at Schönbrunn on the 14th, and in Vienna the following morning.

~ 19 ~

To the Empress, at Strasburg.
Vienna, November 16, 1805.
I am writing to M. d'Harville, so that you can set out and make your way to Baden, then to Stuttgart, and from there to Munich. At Stuttgart you will give the wedding present to the Princess. If it costs fifteen to twenty thousand francs, that will suffice; the rest will do for giving presents at Munich to the daughters of the Electress of Bavaria. All that Madame de Serent has advised you is definitely arranged. Take with you the means to make presents to the ladies and officers who will wait upon you. Be civil, but receive full homage; they owe everything to you, and you owe nothing save civility.

The Electress of Württemberg is daughter of the King of England. She is an excellent woman; you should be very kind to her, but without any affectation. I shall be very glad to see you, the moment circumstances permit me. I'm leaving to join my vanguard. The weather is frightful; it snows heavily. Otherwise my affairs go excellently.

Adieu, my dear.

Napoleon

Madame de Serent. – *Countess de Serent, the Empress's lady in waiting*

They owe everything to you. – *Aubenas quotes this, and remarks (vol. ii. 326): 'No one had pride in France more than Napoleon, stronger even than his conviction of her superiority in the presence of other contemporary sovereigns and courts. He wishes that in Germany, where she will meet families with all the pride and sometimes all the haughtiness of their ancestry, Josephine will not forget that she is Empress of the French, superior to those who are about to receive her, and who owe full respect and homage to her.'*

To the Empress, at Strasburg.

Austerlitz, December 3, 1805.

I have despatched to you Lebrun from the field of battle. I have beaten the Russian and Austrian army commanded by the two Emperors. I am rather tired. I have bivouacked eight days in the open air, through nights sufficiently cold. Tonight I rest in the Château of Prince Kaunitz, where I shall sleep for the next two or three hours. The Russian army is not only beaten, but destroyed.

I embrace you.

Napoleon

Austerlitz. – *Never was a victory more needful; but never was the Emperor more confident. Savary says that it would take a volume to contain all that emanated from his mind during that twenty-four hours (December 1–2). Nor was it confined to military considerations. General Ségur describes how he spent his evening meal with his marshals, discussing with Junot the last new tragedy* (Les Templiers, *by Raynouard), and from it to Racine, Corneille, and the fatalism of our ancestors.*

December 2nd was a veritable Black Monday for the Coalition in general, and for Russia in particular, where Monday is always looked upon as an unlucky day. Their forebodings increased when, on the eve of the battle, the Emperor Alexander was thrown from his horse (Czartoriski, vol. ii. 106).

~ 21 ~

To the Empress, at Munich.

Austerlitz, December 5, 1805.

I have concluded a truce. The Russians have gone. The battle of Austerlitz is the grandest of all I have fought. Forty-five flags, more than 150 cannon, the standards of the Russian Guard, 20 generals, 30,000 prisoners, more than 20,000 slain – a horrible sight.

The Emperor Alexander is in despair, and on his way to Russia. Yesterday, at my bivouac, I saw the Emperor of Germany. We conversed for two hours; we have agreed to make peace quickly. The weather is not now very bad. At last behold peace restored to the Continent; it is to be hoped that it is going to be to the world. The English will not know how to face us.

I look forward with much pleasure to the moment when I can once more be near you. My eyes have been rather bad the last two days; I have never suffered from them before.

Adieu, my dear. I am fairly well, and very anxious to embrace you.

Napoleon

~ 22 ~

To the Empress, at Munich.

Austerlitz, December 7, 1805.

I have concluded an armistice; within a week peace will be made. I am anxious to hear that you reached Munich in good health. The Russians are returning; they have lost enormously – more than 20,000 dead and 30,000 taken. Their army is reduced by three-quarters. Buxhowden, their general-in-chief, was killed. I have 3,000 wounded and 700 to 800 dead.

My eyes are rather bad; it is a prevailing complaint, and scarcely worth mentioning.

Adieu, dear. I am very anxious to see you again.

I am going to sleep tonight at Vienna.

Napoleon

~ 23 ~

To the Empress, at Munich.
Brunn, December 10, 1805.
It is a long time since I had news of you. Have the grand parties at Baden, Stuttgart, and Munich made you forget the poor soldiers, who live covered with mud, rain, and blood?

I shall leave in a few days for Vienna.

We are endeavouring to conclude peace. The Russians have gone, and are in flight far from here; they are on their way back to Russia, well beaten and very much humiliated. I am very anxious to be with you again. Adieu, dear. My bad eyes are cured.

Napoleon

A long time since I had news of you. – *Josephine was always a bad correspondent, but at this juncture was reading that stilted but sensational romance –* Caleb Williams; *or hearing the opera* Achilles *by Paër, or* Romeo and Juliet *by Zingarelli in the intervals of her imperial progress through Germany.*

~ 24 ~

To the Empress, at Munich.
December 19, 1805.
Great Empress,
Not a single letter from you since your departure from Strasburg. You have gone to Baden, Stuttgart, Munich, without writing us a word. This is neither very kind nor very affectionate.

I am still at Brunn. The Russians are gone. I have a truce. In a few days I shall see what I may expect. Deign from the height of your grandeur to concern yourself a little with your slaves.

Napoleon

~ 25 ~

To the Empress, at Munich.

Schönbrunn, December 20, 1805.

I got your letter of the 16th. I am sorry to learn you are in pain. You are not strong enough to travel two hundred and fifty miles at this time of the year. I don't know what I shall do; I await events. I have no will in the matter; everything depends on their issue. Stay at Munich; amuse yourself. That is not difficult when you have so many kind friends and so beautiful a country. I, for my part, am sufficiently busy. In a few days my decision will be made.

Adieu, dear. Kindest and most affectionate regards.

Napoleon

I await events. – *The Treaty of Presburg was soon signed and Napoleon met the Archduke Charles at Stamersdorf, a meeting arranged from mutual esteem. Napoleon had an unswerving admiration for this past and future foe, and said to Madame d'Abrantes, 'That man has a soul, a golden heart'* (Memoirs, *vol.ii. 165). Napoleon, however, did not wish to discuss politics, and only arranged for an interview of two hours, 'one of which', he wrote to Talleyrand, 'will be employed in dining, the other in talking war and in mutual protestations'.*

I, for my part, am sufficiently busy. – *No part of Napoleon's career is more wonderful than the way in which he conducts the affairs of France and of Europe from a hostile capital. But when Napoleon determined, without even consulting his wife, to cement political alliances by matrimonial ones with his and her relatives, he was treading on difficult ground. He wanted a princess for Josephine's son, Eugène, and he preferred Auguste, the daughter of the King of Bavaria. But the young Hereditary Prince of Baden had been accepted by his beautiful cousin Auguste; so, to compensate him for his loss, the pretty and vivacious Stephanie Beauharnais was sent for. For his brother Jerome a bride is found by Napoleon in the daughter of the King of Württemberg. Baden, Bavaria, and Württemberg were too much indebted to France for the spoils they were getting from Austria to object.*

On December 31st, at 1.45 a.m., he entered Munich by torchlight and under a triumphal arch. His chamberlain, M. de Thiard, assured him that if he left Munich the marriage with Eugène would fall through, and he agrees to stay, although he declared that his absence, which accentuated the Bank crisis, is costing him 1,500,000 francs a day. The marriage took place on January 14th, four days after Eugène arrived at Munich and three days after he had shaved off his cherished moustache. Henceforth the bridegroom is called 'Mon fils' in Napoleon's correspondence, and in the contract of marriage Napoleon-Eugène de France. The Emperor and Empress reached the Tuileries on January 27th. The marriage of Stephanie was even more difficult to manage, for, as St. Amand says, the Prince of Baden had for brothers-in-law the Emperor of Russia, the King of Sweden, and the King of Bavaria – two of whom at least were friends of England. Stephanie was the grand-daughter of this couple, and lived until 1860.

~ 26 ~

To The Empress, at Mayence.

October 5, 1806.

It will be quite in order for the Princess of Baden to come to Mayence. I cannot think why you weep; you do wrong to make yourself ill. Hortense is inclined to pedantry; she loves to air her views. She has written me; I am sending her a reply. She ought to be happy and cheerful. Optimism and a merry heart – that's the recipe.

Adieu, dear. The Grand Duke has spoken to me about you; he saw you at Florence at the time of the retreat.

Napoleon

Napoleon left St. Cloud with Josephine on September 25th, and had reached Mayence on the 28th, where his Foot Guard were awaiting him. He left Mayence on October 1st, and reached Würzburg the next day, where this letter was written, just before starting for Bamberg. Josephine was installed in the Teutonic palace at Mayence.

Princess of Baden. – *Stephanie Beauharnais.*

Hortense. – *She was by no means happy with her husband at the best of times, and she cordially hated Holland. She was said to be very frightened of Napoleon, but (like most people) could easily influence her mother. Napoleon's letter to her of this date (October 5th) is certainly not a severe one: 'I have received yours of September 14th. I am sending to the Chief Justice in order to accord pardon to the individual in whom you are interested. Your news always gives me pleasure. I trust you will keep well, and never doubt my great friendship for you.'*

The Grand Duke – *i.e. of Würzburg, brother of Francis, Emperor of Austria.*

Florence. – *Probably September 1796, when Napoleon was hard pressed, and Josephine had to go from Verona to regain Milan, and thus evade Wurmser's troops.*

~ 27 ~

To The Empress, at Mayence.

Bamberg, October 7, 1806.

I start this evening, my dear, for Cronach. The whole of my army is advancing. All goes well. My health is perfect. I have only received as yet one letter from you. I have some from Eugène and from Hortense. Stephanie should now be with you. Her husband wishes to make the campaign; he is with me.

Adieu. A thousand kisses and the best of health.

Napoleon

Bamberg. – *Arriving at Bamberg on the 6th, Napoleon issued a proclamation to his army which concluded – 'Let the Prussian army experience the same fate that it experienced fourteen years ago. Let it learn that, if it is easy to acquire increase of territory and power by means of the friendship of the great people, their enmity, which can be provoked only by the abandonment of all spirit of wisdom and sense, is more terrible than the tempests of the ocean.'*

Eugène. – *Napoleon wrote him on the 5th, and twice on the 7th, on which date we have* eighteen *letters in the* Correspondence.

Her husband. – *The Hereditary Grand Duke of Baden, to whom Napoleon had written from Mayence on September 30th, accepting his services, and fixing the rendezvous at Bamberg for October 4th or 5th.*

On this day Napoleon invaded Prussian territory by entering Bayreuth, having preceded by one day the date of their ultimatum – a document of twenty pages, which Napoleon in his First Bulletin compares to 'one of those which the English Cabinet pay their literary men £500 per annum to write'.

~ 28 ~

To The Empress, at Mayence.

Gera, October 13, 1806, 2 a.m.

My Dear,

I am at Gera today. My affairs go excellently well, and everything as I could wish. With the aid of God, they will, I believe, in a few days have taken a terrible course for the poor King of Prussia, whom I am sorry for personally, because he is a good man. The Queen is at Erfurt with the King. If she wants to see a battle, she shall have that cruel pleasure. I am in splendid health. I have already put on weight since my departure; yet I am doing, in person, twenty and twenty-five leagues a day, on horseback, in my carriage, in all sorts of ways. I lie down at eight, and get up at midnight. I fancy at times that you have not yet gone to bed.

Yours ever, Napoleon

By this time the Prussian army is already in a tight corner, which, as Napoleon says in his Third Bulletin written on this day, is 'assez bizarre, *from which very important events should ensue'. On the previous day he concludes a letter to Talleyrand: 'One cannot conceive how the Duke of Brunswick, to whom one allows some talent, can direct the operations of this army in so ridiculous a manner'.*

Erfurt. – *Here endless discussions, but, as Napoleon says in his bulletin of this day – 'Consternation is at Erfurt, ... but while they deliberate, the French army is marching. ... Still the wishes of the King of Prussia have been executed; he wished that by October 8th the French army should have evacuated the territory of the Confederation which has been evacuated, but in place of retreating over the Rhine, it has advanced over the Saal.'*

If she wants to see a battle. – *Queen Louise was aged thirty in 1806.*

~ 29 ~

To The Empress, at Mayence.

Jena, October 15, 1806, 3 a.m.

My Dear,

I have made excellent manoeuvres against the Prussians. Yesterday I won a great victory. They had 150,000 men. I have made 20,000 prisoners, taken 100 cannon, and flags. I was in presence of the King of Prussia, and near to him; I nearly captured him and the Queen. For the past two days I have bivouacked. I am in excellent health

Adieu, dear. Keep well, and love me.

If Hortense is at Mayence, give her a kiss; also to Napoleon and to the little one.

Napoleon

I nearly captured him and the Queen. – *They escaped by an hour, Napoleon tells Berthier. Blücher aided their escape by telling a French General about an imaginary armistice, which the latter was severely reprimanded by Napoleon for believing. No battle was more beautifully worked out than the battle of Jena. Bernadotte alone, and as usual, gave cause for dissatisfaction. He had a personal dislike for his chief, caused by the knowledge that his wife (Desirée Clary) had never ceased to regret that she had missed her opportunity of being the wife of Napoleon. Bernadotte, therefore, was loath to give initial impetus to the victories of the French Emperor, though, when success was no longer doubtful, he would prove that it was not want of capacity but want of will that had kept him back.*

I have bivouacked. – *Whether the issue of a battle was decisive, or, as at Eylau, only partially so, Napoleon never shunned the disagreeable part of battle – the tending of the wounded and the burial of the dead. Savary tells us that at Jena, as at Austerlitz, the Emperor rode round the field of battle, jumping from his horse with a little brandy flask (constantly refilled), putting his hand to each unconscious soldier's breast, and when he found unexpected life, giving way to a joy 'impossible to describe' (vol. ii. 184).*

~ 30 ~

To The Empress, at Mayence.

Weimar, October 16, 1806, 5 p.m.

M. Talleyrand will have shown you the bulletin, my dear; you will read about my successes in it. All has happened as I calculated, and never was an army more thoroughly beaten and more entirely destroyed. I need only add that I am very well, and that fatigue, bivouacs, and night-watches have made me fat.

Adieu, dear. Kindest regards to Hortense and to the great M. Napoleon.

Yours ever, Napoleon

Fatigues, bivouacs ... have made me fat. – *The Austerlitz campaign had the same effect. See a remarkable letter to Count Miot de Melito on January 30th, 1806: 'The campaign I have just terminated, the movement, the excitement have made me stout. I believe that if all the kings of Europe were to ally against me I should have a ridiculous belly.' And it was so.*

The great M. Napoleon. – *Aged four, and the younger, aged two, are with Hortense and their grandmother at Mayence, where a Court had assembled, including most of the wives of Napoleon's generals, waiting for news.*

~ 31 ~

To The Empress, at Mayence.

Wittenberg, October 23, 1806, noon.

I have received several of your letters. I write you only a line. My affairs prosper. Tomorrow I shall be at Potsdam, and at Berlin on the 25th. I am wonderfully well, and thrive on hard work. I am very glad to hear you are with Hortense and Stephanie, *en grande compagnie*. So far, the weather has been fine.

Kind regards to Stephanie, and to everybody, and not forgetting M. Napoleon.

Adieu, dear.

Yours ever, Napoleon

~ 32 ~

To The Empress, at Mayence.

Potsdam, October 24, 1806.

My Dear,

I have been at Potsdam since yesterday, and shall remain there today. I continue satisfied with my undertakings. My health is good; the weather very fine. I find Sans-Souci very pleasant.

Adieu, dear. Best wishes to Hortense and to M. Napoleon.

Napoleon

Potsdam. – *As a reward for Auerstadt, Napoleon orders Davout and his famous Third Corps to be the first to enter Berlin the following day.*

Sans-Souci. – *Frederick the Great's palace.*

~ 33 ~

To The Empress, at Mayence.

November 1, 1806, 2 a.m.

Talleyrand has just arrived and tells me, my dear, that you do nothing but cry. What on earth do you want? You have your daughter, your grandchildren, and good news; surely these are sufficient reasons for being happy and contented.

The weather here is superb; there has not yet fallen during the whole campaign a single drop of water. I am very well, and all goes excellently.

Adieu, dear; I have received a letter from M. Napoleon; I do not believe it is from him, but from Hortense. Kindest regards to everybody.

Napoleon

Written from Berlin, where he is from October 28th to November 25th.

~ 34 ~

To The Empress, at Mayence.

Berlin, November 2, 1806.

Your letter of October 26th to hand. We have splendid weather here. You will see by the bulletin that we have taken Stettin – it is a very strong place. All my affairs go as well as possible, and I am thoroughly satisfied. One pleasure is alone wanting – that of seeing you, but I hope that will not long be deferred.

Kindest regards to Hortense, Stephanie, and to the little Napoleon. Adieu, dear.

Yours ever, Napoleon

~ 35 ~

To The Empress, at Mayence.

Berlin, Monday, Noon.

My Dear,

I have received your letter. I am glad to know that you are in a place which pleases me, and especially to know that you are very well there.

Who should be happier than you? You should live without a worry, and pass your time as pleasantly as possible; that, indeed, is my intention.

I forbid you to see Madame Tallien, under any pretext whatever. I will admit of no excuse. If you desire a continuance of my respect, if you wish to please me, never transgress the present order. She may possibly come to your apartments, to enter them by night; forbid your porter to admit her.

I shall soon be at Malmaison. I warn you to have no lovers there that night; I should be sorry to disturb them. Adieu, dear; I long to see you and assure you of my love and affection.

Napoleon

Madame Tallien had been in her time, especially in the years 1795-99, one of the most beautiful and witty women in France. Madame d'Abrantes calls her the Venus of the Capital; and Lucien Bonaparte speaks of the court of the voluptuous Director, Barras, where the beautiful Tallien was centre stage. Tallien was, however, celebrated both for her beauty and her intrigues; and when, in 1799, Bonaparte seized supreme power the fair lady burst in on Barras in his bath to inform him of it; but found her indolent patron only capable of saying, 'What can be done? that man has taken us all in!' Napoleon probably remembered this, and may refer to her rather than to the Queen of Prussia in the next letter, where he makes severe strictures on intriguing women. Napoleon knew also that Tallien had been the mistress of Ouvrard, the banker, who in his Spanish speculations a few months earlier had involved the Bank of France to the tune of four millions sterling, and forced Napoleon to make a premature peace after Austerlitz. The Emperor had returned furious to Paris, and wished he could build a gallows for Ouvrard high enough for him to be on view throughout France. Madame Tallien's own father, M. de Cabarrus, was a French banker in Spain, and probably in close contact with Ouvrard.

~ 36 ~

To The Empress, at Mayence.

November 6, 1806, 9 p.m.

Yours to hand, in which you seem annoyed at the bad things I say about women; it is true that I hate intriguing women more than anything. I am used to kind, gentle, persuasive women; these are the kind I like. If I have been spoilt, it is not my fault, but yours. Moreover, you shall learn how kind I have been to one who showed herself sensible and good, Madame Hatzfeld. When I showed her husband's letter to her she admitted to me, amid her sobs, with profound emotion, and frankly, 'Ah! it is indeed his writing!' While she was reading, her voice went to my heart; it pained me. I said, 'Well, Madame, throw that letter on the fire, I shall then have no longer the power to punish your husband.' She burnt the letter, and seemed very happy. Her husband now feels at ease; two hours later he would have been a dead man. You see then how I like kind, frank, gentle women; but it is because such alone resemble you.

Adieu, dear; my health is good.

Napoleon

Written from Berlin.

The bad things I say about women. – *Napoleon looked upon this as a woman's war, and his temper occasionally gets the better of him. In the Fifteenth Bulletin (Wittenberg, October 23rd) he states that the Queen had accused her husband of cowardice in order to bring about the war. But it is doubtless the Sixteenth Bulletin (dated Potsdam, October 25th) to which Josephine refers, and which refers to the oath of alliance of the Emperor Alexander and the King of Prussia in the death chamber of Frederick the Great. 'It is from this moment that the Queen quitted the care of her domestic concerns and the serious occupations of the toilet in order to meddle with the affairs of State.' He refers to a Berlin caricature of the scene which was at the time in all the shops, exciting even the laughter of bumpkins. The handsome Emperor of Russia was portrayed with the Queen of Prussia by his side and on his other side the King of Prussia with his hand raised above the tomb of the Great Frederick; the Queen pressing her hand on her heart, and apparently gazing upon the Emperor of Russia. In the Eighteenth Bulletin (October 26th) it is said the Prussian people did not want war, that a handful of women and young officers had caused it, and that the Queen, 'formerly a timid and modest woman looking after her domestic concerns', had become turbulent and warlike, and had 'conducted the monarchy within a few days to the brink of the precipice'.*

As an antidote, however, to his severe words against women he put, perhaps somewhat ostentatiously, the Princess Hatzfeld episode in his Twenty-second Bulletin (Berlin, October 28th). Prince Hatzfeld had remained in Berlin and had reported on French activity there to the King of Prussia. Napoleon had intercepted the letter and charged the prince with being a spy.

~ 37 ~

To The Empress, at Mayence.

Berlin, November 9, 1806.

My Dear,

I am sending good news. Magdeburg has capitulated, and on November 7th I took 20,000 men at Lubeck who escaped me last week. The whole Prussian army, therefore, is captured; even beyond the Vistula there does not remain to Prussia 20,000 men. Several of my army corps are in Poland. I am still at Berlin. I am very fairly well.

Adieu, dear; heartiest good wishes to Hortense, Stephanie, and the two little Napoleons.

Yours ever, Napoleon

Magdeburg had surrendered on November 8th, with 20 generals, 800 officers and 22,000 men, 800 cannon, and immense stores.

Lubeck. – *This capitulation was that of Blücher, who had escaped after Jena through a rather dishonourable ruse. It had taken three army corps to hem him in.*

~ 38 ~

To The Empress, at Mayence.

Berlin, November 16, 1806.

I received your letter of November 11th. I note with satisfaction that my beliefs give you pleasure. You are wrong to think flattery was intended; I was describing you as I see you. I am grieved to think that you are tired of Mayence. Were the journey less long, you might come here, for there is no longer an enemy, or, if there is, he is beyond the Vistula; that is to say, more than three hundred miles away. I will wait to hear what you think about it. I should also be delighted to see M. Napoleon.

Adieu, my dear.

Yours ever, Napoleon

I have still too much business here for me to return to Paris.

~ 39 ~

To The Empress, at Mayence.

November 22, 1806, 10 p.m.

Your letter received. I am sorry to find you depressed; yet you have every reason to be cheerful. You are wrong to show so much kindness to people who show themselves unworthy of it. Madame L. is a fool; such an idiot that you ought to know her by this time, and pay no heed to her. Be contented, happy in my friendship, and in the great influence you possess. In a few days I shall decide whether to summon you hither or send you to Paris.

Adieu, dear; you can go at once, if you like, to Darmstadt, or to Frankfurt; that will make you forget your troubles.

Kindest regards to Hortense.

Napoleon

Madame de la Rochefoucauld.

Madame Remusat.

Written from Berlin, but not included in the Correspondence.

Madame L., – *Madame de la Rochefoucauld, a third or fourth cousin (by her first marriage) of Josephine, and her chief lady of honour. She was an incorrigible Royalist, and hated Napoleon; but as she had been useful at the Tuileries in establishing the Court, Napoleon, as usual, could not make up his mind to cause her dismissal. In 1806, however, she made Josephine miserable and Mayence unbearable.*

~ 40 ~

To The Empress, at Mayence.

Kustrin, November 26,1806.

I am at Kustrin, making a tour and spying out the land a little; I shall see in a day or two whether you should come. You can keep ready. I shall be very pleased if the Queen of Holland be among the party. The Grand Duchess of Baden must write to her husband about it.

It is 2 a.m. I am just getting up; it is the habit of war.

Kindest regards to you and to every one.

Napoleon

~ 41 ~

To The Empress, at Mayence.

Meseritz, November 27, 1806, 2 a.m.

I am about to make a tour in Poland. This is the first town there. Tonight I shall be at Posen, after which I shall send for you to come to Berlin, so that you can arrive there the same day as I. My health is good, the weather rather bad; it has rained for the past three days. My affairs prosper. The Russians are in flight.

Adieu, dear; kindest regards to Hortense, Stephanie, and the little Napoleons.

Napoleon

~ 42 ~

To The Empress, at Mayence.

Posen, November 29, 1806, noon.

I am at Posen, capital of Great Poland. The cold weather has set in; I am in good health I am about to take a circuit round Poland. My troops are at the gates of Warsaw.

Adieu, dear; very kindest regards, and a hearty embrace.

~ 43 ~

To The Empress, at Mayence.

Posen, December 2, 1806.

Today is the anniversary of Austerlitz. I have been to a city ball. It is raining; I am in good health. I love you and long for you. My troops are at Warsaw. So far the cold has not been severe. All these fair Poles are Frenchwomen at heart; but there is only one woman for me. Would you know her? I could draw her portrait very well; but I should have to flatter it too much for you to recognise yourself; yet, to tell the truth, my heart would only have nice things to say to you. These nights are long, all alone.

Yours ever, Napoleon

~ 44 ~

To The Empress, at Mayence.

December 3, 1806, noon.

Yours of November 26th received. I notice two things in it. You say I do not read your letters: it is an unkind thought. I take your bad opinion anything but kindly. You tell me that perhaps it is a mere whim of the night, and you add that you are not jealous. I found out long ago that angry persons always assert that they are not angry; that those who are afraid keep on repeating that they have no fear; you therefore are convinced of jealousy. I am delighted to hear it! Nevertheless, you are wrong; I think of nothing less, and in the desert plains of Poland one thinks little about beauties. I had yesterday a ball of the provincial nobility – the women good-looking enough, rich enough, dowdy enough, although in Paris fashions.

Adieu, dear; I am in good health.

Yours ever, Napoleon

Jealousy. – *Even though Madame Walewska, Napoleon's Polish mistress, had not yet appeared on the scene.*

~ 45 ~

To The Empress, at Mayence.

Posen, December 3, 1806, 6 p.m.

Yours of November 27th received, from which I see that your little head is quite turned. I am reminded of the verse:

'Desir de femme est un feu qui dévore'.

Still you must calm yourself. I wrote to you that I was in Poland; that, when we were established in winter quarters, you could come; you will have to wait a few days. The more important one becomes, the less one can consult one's wishes being dependent on events and circumstances. You can come to Frankfurt or Darmstadt. I am hoping to send for you in a few days; that is, if circumstances will permit. The warmth of your letter makes me realise that you, like other pretty women, know no bounds. What you will, must be; but, as for me, I declare that of all men I am the greatest slave; my master has no pity, and this master is the nature of things.

Adieu, dear; keep well. The person that I wished to speak to you about is Madame L., of whom every one is speaking ill; they assure me that she is more a Prussian than a French woman. I don't believe it, but I think her an idiot who talks nothing but trash.

Napoleon

~ 46 ~

To The Empress, at Mayence.

Posen, December 9, 1806.

Yours of December 1st received. I see with pleasure that you are more cheerful; that the Queen of Holland wishes to come with you. I long to give the order; but you must still wait a few days. My affairs prosper.

Adieu, dear; I love you and wish to see you happy.

Napoleon

~ 47 ~

To The Empress, at Mayence.

Posen, December 10, 1806, 5 p.m.

An officer has just brought me a rug, a gift from you; it is somewhat short and narrow, but I thank you for it none the less. I am in fair health. The weather is very changeable. My affairs prosper pretty well. I love you and long for you much.

Adieu, dear; I shall write for you to come with at least as much pleasure as you will have in coming.

Yours ever, Napoleon

A kiss to Hortense, Stephanie, and Napoleon.

~ 48 ~

To The Empress, at Mayence.

Posen, December 12th, 1806, 7 p.m.

My Dear,

I have not received any letters from you, but know, nevertheless, that you are well. My health is good, the weather very mild; the bad season has not begun yet, but the roads are bad in a country where there are no highways. Hortense will come then with Napoleon; I am delighted to hear it. I long to sec things shape themselves into a position to enable you to come.

I have made peace with Saxony. The Elector is King and joins the confederation.

Adieu, my well-beloved Josephine.

Yours ever, Napoleon

A kiss to Hortense, Napoleon, and Stephanie.

Paër, the famous musician, his wife, a virtuoso whom you saw at Milan twelve years ago, and Brizzi are here; they give me a little music every evening.

~ 49 ~

To The Empress, at Mayence.

December 15, 1806, 3 p.m.

My Dear,

I'm leaving for Warsaw. In a fortnight I shall be back; I hope then to be able to send for you. But if that seems a long time, I should be very glad if you would return to Paris, where you are wanted. You well know that I am dependent on events. All my affairs go excellently. My health is very good; I am as well as possible.

Adieu, dear. I have made peace with Saxony.

Yours ever, Napoleon

~ 50 ~

To The Empress, at Mayence.

Warsaw, December 20, 1806, 3 p.m.

I have no news from you, dear. I am very well. The last two days I have been at Warsaw. My affairs prosper. The weather is very mild, and even somewhat humid. It has as yet barely begun to freeze; it is October weather.

Adieu, dear; I should much have liked to see you, but trust that in five or six days I shall be able to send for you.

Kindest regards to the Queen of Holland and to her little Napoleons.

Yours ever, Napoleon

~ 51 ~

To The Empress, at Mayence.

Golymin, December 29, 1806, 5 a.m.

I write you only a line, my dear. I am in a wretched barn. I have beaten the Russians, taken thirty cannon, their baggage, and 6,000 prisoners; but the weather is frightful. It is raining; we have mud up to our knees.

In two days I shall be at Warsaw, where I shall write to you.

Yours ever, Napoleon

A wretched barn. – *The Emperor and his horse had nearly been lost in the mud, and Marshal Duroc had a shoulder dislocated when his carriage turned over.*

~ 52 ~

To The Empress, at Mayence.

Pultusk, December 31, 1806.

I have had a good laugh over your last letters. You idealise the beautiful women of Great Poland in a way they do not deserve. I have had for two or three days the pleasure of hearing Paër and two lady singers, who have given me some very good music. I received your letter in a wretched barn, having mud, wind, and straw for my only bed. Tomorrow I shall be at Warsaw. I think all is over for this year. The army is entering winter quarters. I shrug my shoulders at the stupidity of Madame de L.; still you should show her your displeasure, and counsel her not to be so idiotic. Such things become common property, and make many people indignant.

For my part, I scorn ingratitude as the worst fault in a human heart. I know that instead of comforting you, these people have given you pain.

Adieu, dear; I am in good health I do not think you ought to go to Cassel; that place is not suitable. You may go to Darmstadt.

Napoleon

The beautiful women of Great Poland. – *Here is the description of the Duke of Rovigo (vol. ii. 17): 'The stay at Warsaw had for us something bewitching; even with regard to amusements it was practically the same life as at Paris: the Emperor had his concert twice a week, at the end of which he held a reception, where many of the leading people met. A great number of ladies from the best families were admired alike for the brilliancy of their beauty, and for their wonderful friendliness. One may rightly say that the Polish ladies inspired with jealousy the charming women of every other civilised country. They combined to the manners of good society a fund of information which is not commonly found even among Frenchwomen, and is very far above anything we see in towns, where the custom of meeting in public has become a necessity. It seemed to us that the Polish ladies, compelled to spend the greater part of the year in their country-houses, applied themselves there to reading as well as to the cultivation of their talents, and it was thus that in the chief towns, where they went to pass the winter, they appeared successful over all their rivals.' Josephine was right to be jealous, for, as the artist Baron Lejeune adds, 'They were, moreover, as graceful as the Creole women so often are.'*

Such things become common property. – *So was another event, much to*

Josephine's consternation. On this date Napoleon heard of a son (Leon) born to him by Eléanore, a former schoolfellow of Madame Murat.

~ 53 ~

To The Empress, at Mayence.

Warsaw, January 3, 1807.

My Dear,

I have received your letter. Your grief pains me; but one must bow to events. There is too much country to travel between Mayence and Warsaw; you must therefore, wait until circumstances allow me to come to Berlin, so that I can write to you to come and join me. It is true that the enemy, defeated, is far away; but I still have many things here to put to rights. I should be inclined to think that you might return to Paris, where you are needed. Send away those ladies who have their affairs to look after; you will be better without people who have given you so much worry.

My health is good; the weather bad. I love you from my heart.

Napoleon

Warsaw, January 3. – *On his way from Pultusk on January 1, he had received a Polish ovation at Bronie, where he first met Madame Walewska. The whole story is well told by M. Masson in* Napoleon et les Femmes; *but here we must content ourselves with the mere facts, and first, for the sake of comparison, cite his love-letters to the lady in question: (1) 'I have seen only you, I have admired only you, I desire only you. A very prompt answer to calm the impatient ardour of N.' (2) 'Have I displeased you? I have still the right to hope to the contrary. Have I been mistaken? Your eagerness diminishes, while mine augments. You take away my rest! Oh, give a little joy, a little happiness to a poor heart all ready to worship you. Is it so difficult to get a reply? You owe me one. – N.' (3) 'There are moments when too high rank is a burden, and that is what I feel. How can I satisfy the needs of a heart hopelessly in love, which would fling itself at your feet, and which finds itself stopped by the weight of lofty considerations paralysing the most lively desires? Oh, if you would! Only you could remove the obstacles that lie between us. My friend Duroc will clear the way. Oh, come! come! All your wishes shall be gratified. Your native land will be dearer to me when you have had pity on my poor heart. – N.' (4) 'Marie, my sweet Marie ! My first thought is for you, my first desire to see you again. You will come again, will you not? You promised me to do so. If not, the eagle will fly to you. I shall see you at dinner, a friend tells me. Deign, then, to accept this bouquet; let it become a mysterious link which shall establish between us a secret union in the midst of the crowd surrounding us. Exposed to the glances of the crowd, we shall still understand each other. When my hand presses my heart, you will know that it is full of thoughts of you; and in answer you will press closer your bouquet. Love me, my pretty Marie, and never let your hand leave your bouquet. – N.' In this letter, in which he has substituted* tu *for* vous, *there is more passion than we have seen since 1796. The fair lady now leaves her decrepit old husband, nearly fifty years her senior, and takes up her abode in Finckenstein Castle, for nearly two months of the interval between Eylau and Friedland. Napoleon confessed to Lucien at Mantua a few months later that 'her soul was as beautiful as her face'. Napoleon's letters from Warsaw betray a certain unease that his affair might become known to Josephine.*

To The Empress, at Mayence.
Warsaw, January 7, 1807.
My Dear,
I am pained by all that you tell me; but the season being cold, the roads very bad and not at all safe, I cannot consent to expose you to so many fatigues and dangers. Return to Paris in order to spend the winter there. Go to the Tuileries; receive, and lead the same life as you are accustomed to do when I am there; that is my wish. Perhaps I shall not be long in rejoining you there; but it is absolutely necessary for you to give up the idea of making a journey of 750 miles at this time of

the year, through the enemy's country, and in the rear of the army. Believe that it costs me more than you to put off for some weeks the pleasure of seeing you, but events and the success of my plans order it.

Adieu, my dear; be cheerful, and show character.

Napoleon

~ 55 ~

To The Empress, at Mayence.

Warsaw, January 8, 1807.

My Dear,

I received your letter of the 27th with those of M. Napoleon and Hortense, which were enclosed with it. I had begged you to return to Paris. The weather is too bad, the roads unsafe and detestable; the distances too great for me to permit you to come here, where my affairs detain me. It would take you at least a month to come. You would arrive ill; by that time it might perhaps be necessary to start back again; it would therefore be foolish to try. Your residence at Mayence is too dull; Paris reclaims you; go there, it is my wish. I am more cross about it than you. I should have liked to spend the long nights of this season with you, but we must obey circumstances.

Adieu, dear.

Yours ever, Napoleon

~ 56 ~

To The Empress, at Mayence.

Warsaw, January 11, 1807.

Your letter of the 27th received, from which I note that you are somewhat uneasy about military events. Everything is settled, as I have told you, to my satisfaction; my affairs prosper. The distance is too great for me to allow you to come so far at this time of year. I am in splendid health, sometimes rather wearied by the length of the nights.

Up to the present I have seen few people here.

Adieu, dear. I wish you to be cheerful, and to give a little life to the capital. I would much like to be there.

Yours ever, Napoleon

I hope that the Queen has gone to The Hague with M. Napoleon.

~ 57 ~

To The Empress, at Mayence.

January 16, 1807.

My Dear,

I have received your letter of the 5th of January; all that you tell me of your unhappiness pains me. Why these tears, this depression? Have you not got any strength? I shall see you soon. Never doubt my feelings; and if you wish to be still dearer to me, show character and strength of mind. I am humiliated to think that my wife can distrust my destinies.

Adieu, dear. I love you, I long to see you, and wish to learn that you are content and happy.

Napoleon

~ 58 ~

To The Empress, at Mayence.

Warsaw, January 18, 1807.

I fear that you are greatly grieved at our separation and at your return to Paris, which must last for some weeks longer. I insist on you having more strength. I hear you are always weeping. For goodness' sake! How bad this is! Your letter of January 7 makes me unhappy. Be worthy of me; assume more character. Cut a suitable figure at Paris; and, above all, be happy.

I am very well, and I love you much; but, if you are always crying, I shall think you without courage and without character. I do not love cowards. An Empress ought to show some will power.

Napoleon

~ 59 ~

To The Empress, at Mayence.
Warsaw, January 19, 1807.
My Dear,
Your letter to hand.

I have laughed at your fear of fire.

I am in despair at the tone of your letters and at what I hear. I forbid you to weep, to be petulant and worried; I desire that you be cheerful, lovable, and happy.

Napoleon

~ 60 ~

To The Empress, at Mayence.
Warsaw, January 23, 1807.
Your letter of January 15th has arrived. It is impossible to allow women to make such a journey as this – bad roads, muddy and unsafe. Return to Paris; be cheerful and content there. Perhaps even I shall soon be there.

I have laughed at what you say about you having married a husband so that you can be with him. I thought, in my ignorance, that the wife was made for the husband, the husband for his country, his family, and glory. Pardon my ignorance; one is always learning from pretty ladies.

Adieu, my dear. Think how much it costs me not to have you here. Say to yourself, 'It is a proof how precious I am to him'.

Napoleon

~ 61 ~

To The Empress, at Mayence.
January 25, 1807.
I am very unhappy to see you are in pain. I hope that you are at Paris; you will get better there. I share your grief, and do not groan. For I could not risk losing you by exposing you to fatigues and dangers which befit neither your rank nor your sex.

I wish you never to receive T. at Paris; he is a black sheep. You would grieve me by doing otherwise.

Adieu, my dear. Love me, and be courageous.

Napoleon

Written from Warsaw, and omitted from the Correspondence.

T. – *Is Tallien, who had misbehaved himself in Egypt. Madame Junot met him at Madrid, but she and others had not forgotten the September massacres.* '

~ 62 ~

To The Empress, at Paris.
Warsaw, January 26, 1807, noon.
My Dear,
I have received your letter. It pains me to see how you are worrying yourself. The bridge of Mayence neither increases nor decreases the distance which separates us. Remain, therefore, at Paris. I should be troubled and uneasy to know that you were so miserable and so isolated at Mayence. You must know that I need to concentrate only on the success of my enterprise. If I could consult my heart I should be with you, or you with me; for you would be most unjust if you doubted my love and entire affection.

Napoleon

Paris. – *Josephine arrived here January 31st; Queen Hortense going to The Hague and the Princess Stephanie to Mannheim.*

~ 63 ~

To The Empress, at Paris.

Willenberg, February 1, 1807, noon.

Your letter of the 11th, from Mayence, has made me laugh.

Today, I am a hundred miles from Warsaw; the weather is cold, but fine.

Adieu, dear; be happy, show character.

Napoleon

~ 64 ~

To The Empress, at Paris.

My Dear,

Your letter of January 20th has given me pain; it is too sad. That's the fault of not being a sufficient believer! You tell me that your glory consists in your happiness. That is narrow-minded; one should say, my glory consists in the happiness of others. It is not what one says in marriage; one should say, my glory consists in the happiness of my husband. It is not maternal; one should say, my glory consists in the happiness of my children. Now, since nations – your husband, your children – can only be happy with a certain amount of glory, you must not make fun of it. Josephine! your heart is excellent and your arguments weak. You feel acutely, but you don't argue as well.

That's sufficient quarrelling. I want you to be cheerful, happy with your role, and that you should obey, not with grumbling and tears, but with gaiety of heart and a little more good temper.

Adieu, dear; I'm leaving tonight to examine my outposts.

Napoleon

Probably written from Arensdorf, on the eve of the battle of Eylau (February 9th), on which day a great ball took place in Paris, given by the Minister of Marine.

~ 65 ~

To The Empress, at Paris.

Eylau, February 9, 1807, 3 a.m.

My Dear,

Yesterday there was a great battle; the victory is mine, but I have lost many men. The loss of the enemy, which is still more considerable, does not console me. To conclude, I write you these two lines myself, although I am very tired, to tell you that I am well and that I love you.

Yours ever, Napoleon

Eylau. – *The battle of Preussich-Eylau was stubbornly fought on both sides, but the Russian general, Beningsen, had all the luck: (1) His Cossacks capture Napoleon's letter to Bernadotte, which enables him to escape all Napoleon's plans, which otherwise would have destroyed half the Russian army. (2) A snowstorm in the middle of the day in the faces of the French ruins Augereau's corps and saves the Russians from a total rout. (3) The arrival of a Prussian army corps, under General Lestocq, robbed Davout of victory on the right, and much of the ground gained – including the village of Kuschnitten. (4) The night came on just in time to save the rest of the Russian army, and to prevent Ney taking any decisive part in the battle. The forces, according to Matthieu Dumas (*Précis des Evenements Militaires, *volume 18), were approximately 65,000 French against 80,000 allies (Alison says 75,000 allies, 85,000 French, but admits the allies had 100 more cannon) – the latter in a strong chosen position. The allies lost 5,000 to 6,000 dead and 20,000 wounded. Napoleon told Montholon that his loss at Eylau was 18,000, which probably included 2,000 dead, and 15,000 to 16,000 wounded and prisoners.*

~ 66 ~

To The Empress, at Paris.

Eylau, February 9, 1807, 6 p.m.

My Dear,

I write you a line in order that you may not be uneasy. The enemy has lost the battle, 40 cannon, 10 flags, 12,000 prisoners; he has suffered frightfully. I have lost many: 1,600 killed, 3,000 or 4,000 wounded.

Your cousin Tascher conducts himself well; I have summoned him near me with the title of orderly officer.

Corbineau has been killed by a shell; I was singularly attached to that officer, who had much merit; I am very unhappy about him. My horse guard has covered itself with glory. Dahlman is dangerously wounded.

Adieu, dear.

Yours ever, Napoleon

Corbineau. – *Claude Corbineau (1772-1807) was Josephine's equerry and was promoted to General in 1806.*

Dahlman. – *General Nicholas Dahlman (1769-1807), commanding the chasseurs of the guard, was killed in the charge on the Russian infantry which saved the battle. On April 22nd Napoleon wrote to Vice Admiral Decrés to have three frigates put on the stocks to be called* Dahlman, Corbineau *and* Hautpoul, *and in each captain's cabin a marble inscription recounting their brave deeds.*

~ 67 ~

To The Empress, at Paris.

Eylau, February 11, 1807, 3 a.m.

My Dear,

I write you a line; you must have been very anxious. I have beaten the enemy in a fight to be remembered, but it has cost many brave lives. The bad weather that has set in forces me to take cantonments.

Do not make yourself suffer, please; all this will soon be over, and the happiness of seeing you will make me promptly forget my fatigues. Besides, I have never been in better health.

Young Tascher, of the 4th Regiment, has behaved well; he has had a rough time of it. I have summoned him near me; I have made him an orderly officer – there's an end to his troubles. This young man interests me.

Adieu, dear; a thousand kisses.

Napoleon

Young Tascher. – *The third of Josephine's cousins of that name. He was afterwards the aide-de-camp of Prince Eugène, and later major-domo of the Empress Eugénie.*

~ 68 ~

To The Empress, at Paris.

Preussich-Eylau, February 12, 1807.

I send you a letter from General Darmagnac. He is a very good soldier, who commanded the 32nd. He is much attached to me. If this Madame de Richmond be well off, and it is a good match, I shall see this marriage with pleasure. Make this known to both of them.

Napoleon

~ 69 ~

To The Empress, at Paris.

Eylau, February 14, 1807.

My Dear,

I am still at Eylau. This country is covered with dead and wounded. It is not the bright side of warfare; one suffers, and the mind is oppressed at the sight of so many victims. My health is good. I have done as I wished, and driven back the enemy, while making his projects fail.

You are sure to be worried, and that thought troubles me. Nevertheless, calm yourself, my dear, and be cheerful.

Yours, Napoleon

Tell Caroline and Pauline that the Grand Duke and the Prince are in excellent health

I am still at Eylau. – *It took Napoleon and his army eight days to bury the dead and remove the wounded. Lejeune says, 'His whole time was given up now to seeing that the wounded received proper care, and he insisted on the Russians being as well treated as the French' (vol. i. 48). The Emperor wrote to Daru that if more surgeons had been on the spot he could have saved at least 200 lives. A few days later Napoleon tells Daru on no account to begrudge money for medicines, and especially for quinine.*

This country is covered with dead and wounded. – *'Napoleon', says Dumas (vol. i. 18, 41), 'having given the order that the aid to the wounded on both sides might be multiplied, rode over the field of battle, which all eyewitnesses agree to have been the most horrible field of carnage which war has ever offered. In a space of less than a square league, the ground covered with snow, and the frozen lakes, were heaped up with 10,000 dead, and 3,000 to 4,000 dead horses, debris of artillery, arms of all kinds, cannonballs, and shells. Six thousand Russians, expiring of their wounds, and of hunger and thirst, were left abandoned to the generosity of the conqueror.'*

Grand Duke and the Prince. – *Murat, Grand Duke of Berg, and Prince Borghèse, Pauline Bonaparte's rich, but diminutive, husband.*

~ 70 ~

To The Empress, at Paris.

Eylau, February 17, 1807, 3 a.m.

Your letter to hand, informing me of your arrival at Paris. I am very glad to know you are there. My health is good.

The battle of Eylau was very bloody, and sternly contested.

Corbineau was slain. He was a very brave man. I had grown very fond of him.

Adieu, dear; it is as warm here as in the month of April; everything is thawing. My health is good.

Napoleon

~ 71 ~

To The Empress, at Paris.
Landsberg, February 18, 1807, 3 a.m.
I write you two lines. My health is good. I am moving to get my army into winter quarters.

It rains and thaws as in the month of April. We have not yet had one cold day.

Adieu, dear.

Yours ever, Napoleon

~ 72 ~

To The Empress, at Paris.
Liebstadt, February 20, 1807, 2 a.m.
I write you two lines, dear, in order that you may not be uneasy. My health is very good, and my affairs prosper.

I have again put my army into cantonments.

The weather is extraordinary; it freezes and thaws; it is wet and unsettled.

Adieu, dear.

Yours ever, Napoleon

~ 73 ~

To The Empress, at Paris.
Liebstadt, February 21, 1807, 2 a.m.
Your letter of the 4th February to hand; I see with pleasure that your

health is good. Paris will thoroughly re-establish it by giving you cheerfulness and rest, and a return to your accustomed habits.

I am wonderfully well. The weather and the country are vile. My affairs are fairly satisfactory. It thaws and freezes within twenty-four hours; there can never have been known such an extraordinary winter.

Adieu, dear; I love you, I think of you, and wish to know that you are contented, cheerful, and happy.

Yours ever, Napoleon

~ 74 ~

To The Empress, at Paris.
Liebstadt, February 21, 1807, noon.
My Dear,
Your letter of the 8th received; I see with pleasure that you have been to the opera, and that you propose holding receptions weekly. Go occasionally to the theatre, and always into the Royal box. I notice also with pleasure the banquets you are giving.

I am very well. The weather is still unsettled; it freezes and thaws. I have once more put my army into cantonments in order to rest them.

Never be doleful, love me, and believe in my entire affection.

Napoleon

~ 75 ~

To The Empress, at Paris.
Osterode, February 23, 1807, 2 p.m.
My Dear,
Your letter of the 10th received. I am sorry to see you are a little out of sorts.

I have been in the country for the past month, experiencing frightful weather, because it has been unsettled, and varying from cold to warm within a week. Still, I am very well.

Try and pass your time pleasantly; have no anxieties, and never doubt the love I bear you.

Napoleon

~ 76 ~

To The Empress, at Paris.

Osterode, March 2, 1807.

My Dear,

It is two or three days since I wrote to you; I reproach myself for it; I know your uneasiness. I am very well; my affairs prosper. I am in a wretched village, where I shall pass a considerable time; it is not as good as the great city! I again assure you, I was never in such good health; you will find me very much fatter.

It is spring weather here; the snow has gone, the streams are thawing – which is what I want.

I have ordered what you wish for Malmaison; be cheerful and happy; it is my command.

Adieu, dear; I embrace you heartily.

Yours ever, Napoleon

Osterode. – *'A wretched village, where I shall pass a considerable time'. Savary speaks of him there, 'working, eating, giving audience, and sleeping – all in the same room', alone against the opinions of his marshals, who wished him to retire across the Vistula. He remained at Osterode more than five weeks and more than two months at Finckenstein Castle, interesting himself in the affairs of Tehran and Montevideo, offering prizes for discoveries in electricity and medicine, giving advice as to the best scientific methods of teaching history and geography, whilst objecting to the creation of poet-laureates whose exaggerated praises would be sure to awaken the ridicule of the French people.*

It is not as good as the great city. – *The day before he had written to his brother Joseph that neither his officers nor his staff had taken their clothes off for two months; that he had not taken his boots off for a fortnight; that the wounded had to be moved 120 miles in sledges, in the open air; that bread was not to be had; that the Emperor had been living for weeks upon potatoes, and the officers upon meat. 'After having destroyed the Prussian monarchy, we are fighting against the remnant of the Prussians, against Russians, Cossacks, and Kalmucks, those roving tribes of the north, who formerly invaded the Roman Empire.'*

~ 77 ~

To The Empress, at Paris.
Osterode, March 10, 1807, 4 p.m.
My Dear,
I have received your letter of the 25th. I see with pleasure that you are well, and that you sometimes make a pilgrimage to Malmaison.

My health is good, and my affairs prosper. The weather has become rather cold again. I see that the winter has been very variable everywhere.

Adieu, dear; keep well, be cheerful, and never doubt my affection.

Yours ever, Napoleon

~ 78 ~

To The Empress, at Paris.
Osterode, March 11, 1807.
My Dear,
I received your letter of the 27th. I am sorry to see from it that you are ill; take courage. My health is good; my affairs prosper. I am waiting for fine weather, which should soon be here. I love you and want to know that you are content and cheerful.

A great deal of nonsense will be talked of the battle of Eylau; the bulletin tells everything; our losses are actually exaggerated in it than minimised.

Yours ever, Napoleon

~ 79 ~

To The Empress, at Paris.

Osterode, March 13, 1807, 2 p.m.

My Dear,

I learn that the troublesome gossip that occurred in your salon at Mayence has begun again; make people hold their tongues. I shall be seriously annoyed with you if you do not find a remedy. You allow yourself to be worried by the chatter of people who ought to console you. I desire you to have a little character, and to know how to put everybody into his (or her) proper place.

I am in excellent health. My affairs here are good. We are resting a little, and organising our food supply.

Adieu, dear; keep well.

Napoleon

~ 80 ~

To The Empress, at Paris.

Osterode, March 15, 1807.

I received your letter of the 1st of March, from which I see that you were much upset by the catastrophe of Minerva at the opera. I am very glad to see that you go out and seek distractions.

My health is very good. My affairs go excellently. Take no heed of all the unfavourable rumours that may be circulated. Never doubt my affection, and be without the least uneasiness.

Yours ever, Napoleon

Minerva. – *In a letter of March 7th Josephine writes to Hortense: 'A few days ago I saw a frightful accident at the Opera. The actress who represented Minerva in the ballet of* Ulysses *fell twenty feet and broke her arm. As she is poor and has a family to support, I have sent her fifty louis.' This was probably the ballet,* The Return of Ulysses, *a subject given by Napoleon to Fouché as a suitable subject for representation. In the same letter Josephine writes: 'All the private letters I have received agree in saying that the Emperor was very much exposed at the battle of Eylau. I get news of him very often, sometimes two letters a day, but that does not replace him.' This special danger at Eylau is told by Las Cases, who heard it from Bertrand. Napoleon was on foot, with only a few officers of his staff; a column of four to five thousand Russians broke through towards them. Berthier instantly ordered up the horses. The Emperor gave him a reproachful look; then sent orders to a battalion of his guard to advance, which was a good way behind, and standing still. As the Russians advanced he repeated several times, 'What audacity, what audacity!'. At the sight of his Grenadiers of the Guard the Russians stopped short. It was high time for them to do so, as Bertrand said. The Emperor never moved; all who surrounded him had been much alarmed.*

~ 81 ~

To The Empress, at Paris.
Osterode, March 17, 1807.
My Dear,
It is not necessary for you to go to the small plays and into a private box; it ill befits your rank; you should only go to the four great theatres, and always into the Royal box. Live as you would do if I were at Paris.

My health is very good. The cold weather has recommenced. The thermometer has been down to 8°.

Yours ever, Napoleon

~ 82 ~

To The Empress, at Paris.
Osterode, March 17, 1807, 10 p.m.
I have received yours of March 5th, from which I see with pleasure that you are well. My health is perfect. Yet the weather of the past two days has been cold again; the thermometer tonight has been at 10°,

but the sun has given us a very fine day.

Adieu, dear. Very kindest regards to everybody. Tell me something about the death of that poor Dupuis; have his brother told that I wish to help him. My affairs here go excellently.

Yours ever, Napoleon

Dupuis. – *Former principal of the Brienne Military School. Napoleon, always solicitous for the happiness of those whom he had known in his youth, had made Dupuis his own librarian at Malmaison. His brother, who died in 1809, was the learned Egyptologist.*

~ 83 ~

To The Empress, at Paris.
March 25, 1807.
I have received your letter of March 13th. If you really wish to please me, you must live exactly as you live when I am at Paris. Then you were not in the habit of visiting the second rate theatres or other places. You ought always to go into the Royal box.

As for your home life: hold receptions there, and have your fixed circles of friends; that, my dear, is the only way to deserve my approbation. Greatness has its inconveniences; an Empress cannot go where a private individual may.

Very best love. My health is good. My affairs prosper.

Napoleon

~ 84 ~

To The Empress, at Paris.
Osterode, March 27, 1807, 7 p.m.
My Dear,
Your letter pains me. There is no question of your dying. You are in good health, and you can have no just ground for grief.

I think you should go during May to St. Cloud; but you must spend the whole month of April at Paris.

My health is good. My affairs prosper.

You must not think of travelling this summer; nothing of that sort is feasible. You ought not to frequent inns and camps. I long as much as you for our meeting and for a quiet life.

I can do other things besides fight; but duty stands first and foremost. All my life I have sacrificed everything – peace of mind, personal advantage, happiness – to my destiny.

Adieu, dear. See as little as possible of that Madame de P. She is a woman who belongs to the lowest grade of society; she is thoroughly common and vulgar.

Napoleon

I have had occasion to find fault with M. de T. I have sent him to his country house in Burgundy. I wish no longer to hear his name mentioned.

M. de T. – *Monsieur de Thiard. In* Lettres Inedites de Napoleon I *(Brotonne), No. 176, to Talleyrand, March 22nd, the Emperor writes: 'I have had M. de Thiard struck off from the list of officers. I have sent him away, after having told him all my displeasure, and ordered him to stay on his estate. He is a man without military honour and civic fidelity ... My intention is that he shall also be struck off from the number of my chamberlains. I have been poignantly grieved at such black ingratitude, but I think myself fortunate to have found out such a wicked man in time.' De Thiard seems to have been corresponding with the Russians from Warsaw.*

~ 85 ~

To The Empress, at Paris.
Osterode, April 1, 1807.
My Dear,
I have just got your letter of the 20th I am sorry to see you are ill. I told you to stay at Paris the whole month of April, and to go to St. Cloud on May 1st. You may go and spend the Sundays, and a day or two, at Malmaison. At St. Cloud you may have your usual visitors.

My health is good. It is still quite cold enough here. All is quiet.

I have named the little princess Josephine. Eugène should be well pleased.

Yours ever, Napoleon

Princess Josephine. – *Eugène's eldest daughter, Princess Josephine Maximilliene Auguste, born March 14, 1807; she married Bernadotte's son, Prince Oscar.*

~ 86 ~

To The Empress, at Paris.
Finckenstein, April 2, 1807.
My Dear,
I write you a line. I have just moved my headquarters into a very fine château, after the style of Bessières', where I have several fireplaces, which is a great comfort to me; getting up often in the night, I like to see the fire.

My health is perfect. The weather is fine, but still cold. The thermometer is at four to five degrees.

Adieu, dear.

Yours ever, Napoleon

Bessières. – *His château of Grignon, now destroyed, was one of the most beautiful of Provence.*

~ 87 ~

To The Empress, at Paris.
Finckenstein, April 6, 1807, 3 p.m.
My Dear,
I have received your letter, from which I see you have spent Holy Week at Malmaison, and that your health is better. I long to hear that you are thoroughly well.

I am in a fine château, where there are fireplaces, which I find a great comfort. It is still very cold here; everything is frozen.

You will have seen that I have good news from Constantinople.

My health is good. There is nothing new here.

Yours ever, Napoleon

Constantinople. – *The French envoy, Sebastiani, had managed to turn the Turks against the British. This would lead to the defeat of a British squadron in the Dardanelles in May and a British defeat in Egypt.*

~ 88 ~

To The Empress, at Paris.
Finckenstein, April 10, 1807, 6 p.m.
My Dear,
My health is excellent. Here spring is beginning; but as yet there is no vegetation. I wish you to be cheerful and contented, and never to doubt my attachment. Here all goes well.

Napoleon

~ 89 ~

To The Empress, at Paris.
Finckenstein, April 14, 1807, 7 p.m.
I have received your letter of April 3rd. I see from it that you are well, and that it has been very cold in Paris. The weather here is very

unsettled; still I think the spring has come at length; already the ice has almost gone. I am in splendid health.

Adieu, dear. I ordered some time ago for Malmaison all that you ask for.

Yours ever, Napoleon

~ 90 ~

To The Empress, at Paris.

Finckenstein, April 18, 1807.

I have received your letter of April 5th. I am sorry to see from it that you are grieved at what I have told you. As usual, your little Creole head becomes scatty and excited in a moment. Let us not, therefore, speak of it again. I am very well, but yet the weather is rainy. Savary is very ill of a fever near Danzig; I hope it will be nothing serious.

Adieu, dear; my very best wishes to you.

Napoleon

~ 91 ~

To The Empress, at Paris.

Finckenstein, April 24, 1807, 7 p.m.

I have received your letter of the 12th. I see from it that your health is good, and that you are very happy at the thought of going to Malmaison. The weather has changed to fine; I hope it may continue so.

There is nothing fresh here. I am very well.

Adieu, dear.

Yours ever, Napoleon

~ 92 ~

To The Empress, at Paris.
Finckenstein, May 2, 1807, 4 p.m.
My Dear,
I have just received your letter of the 23rd; I see with pleasure that you are well, and that you are as fond as ever of Malmaison. I hear the Arch-Chancellor is in love. Is this a joke, or a fact? It has amused me; you might have given me a hint about it!

I am very well, and the fine season commences. Spring shows itself at length, and the leaves begin to shoot.

Adieu, dear; very best wishes.

Yours ever, Napoleon

~ 93 ~

To The Empress, at Paris.
Finckenstein, May 10, 1807.
I have just received your letter. I don't know what you are saying about ladies in your correspondence with me. I love only my little Josephine, sweet, pouting, and capricious, who can quarrel with grace, as she does everything else, for she is always lovable, except when she is jealous; then she becomes a real little devil [toute diablesse]. But let us come back to these ladies. If I had the time for any of them, I assure you that I should like them to be pretty rosebuds. Are those of whom you speak like that?

I wish you to have only those persons to dinner who have dined with me; that your list be the same for your assemblies; that you never make intimates at Malmaison of ambassadors and foreigners. If you should do the contrary, you would displease me. Finally, do not allow yourself to be duped too much by persons whom I do not know, and who would not come to the house, if I were there.

Adieu, dear.

Yours ever, Napoleon

The palace of Saint Cloud.

~ 94 ~

To The Empress, at Paris.

Finckenstein, May 12, 1807.

I have just received your letter of May 2nd, in which I see that you are getting ready to go to St. Cloud. I was sorry to see the bad conduct of Madame…. Might you not speak to her about mending her ways, which at present might easily cause unpleasantness on the part of her husband?

From what I hear, Napoleon is cured; I can well imagine how unhappy his mother has been; but measles is an ailment to which every one is liable. I hope that he has been vaccinated, and that he will at least be safe from the smallpox.

Adieu, dear. The weather is very warm, and vegetation has begun; but it will be some days before there is any grass.

Napoleon

Madame. – *His own sister, Caroline Murat, afterwards Queen of Naples, was flirting with General Junot.*

Measles. – *As Hortense's poor child was ill four days, it was probably laryngitis from which he would die – an ailment hardly distinguishable from croup, and one of the commonest sequelæ of measles.*

~ 95 ~

To The Empress, at St. Cloud.

Finckenstein, May 14, 1807.

I realise the grief which the death of this poor Napoleon must cause you; you can imagine what I am enduring. I should like to be by your side, in order that your sorrow might be kept within reasonable bounds. You have had the good fortune never to lose children; but it is one of the pains and conditions attached to our miseries here below. I trust I may hear you have been rational in your sorrow, and that your health remains good! Would you willingly augment my grief?

Adieu, dear.

Napoleon

Charles Napoleon, Prince Royal of Holland, died at The Hague on May 5th 1807. The best account is the Memoirs *of Stanislaus Giraudin. They had applied leeches to the child's chest, and had finally recourse to some English powders of unknown composition, which caused a rally, followed by the final collapse. King Louis said the child's death was caused by the Dutch damp climate, which was bad for his own health. Josephine hastens to join her daughter, but breaks down at Lacken, where Hortense, more dead than alive, joins her, and returns to Paris with her.*

I trust I may hear you have been rational in your sorrow. – *As a matter of fact he had heard the opposite, for the following day he writes to his brother Jerome: 'Napoleon died in three days at The Hague; I don't know if the King has advised you of it. This event gives me the more pain insomuch as his father and mother are not rational, and are giving themselves up to all the transports of their grief.' To Fouché he writes three days later: 'I have been very much afflicted by the misfortune which has befallen me. I had hoped for a more brilliant destiny for that poor child' and on May 20th, 'I have felt the loss of the little Napoleon very acutely. I would have wished that his father and mother should have received from their temperament as much courage as I for knowing how to bear all the ills of life. But they are younger, and have reflected less on the frailty of our worldly possessions.'*

~ 96 ~

To The Empress, at St. Cloud.

Finckenstein, May 16, 1807.

I have just received your letter of May 6th. I see from it how ill you are already; and I fear that you are not rational, and that you are making yourself too wretched about the misfortune which has come upon us.

Adieu, dear.

Yours ever, Napoleon

~ 97 ~

To The Empress, at Lacken.

Finckenstein, May 20, 1807.

I have just received your letter of May 10th. I see that you have gone to Lacken. I think you might stay there a fortnight; it would please the Belgians and serve to distract you.

I am sorry to see that you have not been rational. Grief has bounds which should not be passed. Take care of yourself for the sake of your friend, and believe in my entire affection.

Napoleon

May 20th. – *On this date he writes to Hortense: 'My daughter, all the news I get from The Hague tells me that you are not rational. However legitimate your grief, it must have limits: never impair your health; seek distractions, and know that life is strewn with so many rocks, and may be the source of so many miseries, that death is not the greatest of all. Your affectionate father, Napoleon.'*

~ 98 ~

To The Empress, at Lacken.

Finckenstein, May 24, 1807.

Your letter from Lacken just received. I am sorry to see your grief undiminished, and that Hortense has not yet come; she is unreasonable, and does not deserve our love, since she only loves her children.

Try to calm her, and do not make me wretched. For every ill without a cure some consolation must be found.

Adieu, dear.

Yours ever, Napoleon

~ 99 ~

To The Empress, at Lacken.

Finckenstein, May 26, 1807.

I have just received your letter of the 16th. I have seen with pleasure that Hortense has arrived at Lacken. I am annoyed at what you tell me of the state in which she still is. She must have more courage, and force herself to have it.

I cannot imagine why they want her to go to take the waters; she will forget her trouble much better at Paris, and find more sources of consolation.

Show force of character, be cheerful, and keep well. My health is excellent.

Adieu, dear. I suffer much from all your grief; it is a great trouble to me not to be by your side.

Napoleon

~ 100 ~

To The Empress, at Malmaison.

Danzig, June 2, 1807.

My Dear,

I note your arrival at Malmaison. I have no letters from you; I am cross with Hortense, she has never written me a line. All that you tell me about her grieves me. Why have you not found her some distractions? Weeping won't do! I trust you will take care of yourself in order that I may not find you utterly lost.

I have been the two past days at Danzig; the weather is very fine, my health excellent. I think more of you than you are thinking of a husband far away.

Adieu, dear; very kindest regards. Pass on this letter to Hortense.

I am cross with Hortense. – *The same day he writes to Hortense. 'My daughter, you have not written me a line during your great and righteous grief. You have forgotten everything, as if you had nothing more to lose. They say you care no longer for any one, that you are callous about everything; I note the truth of it by your silence. This is not well, Hortense, it is not what you promised me. Your son was everything for you. Are your mother and myself nothing? Had I been at Malmaison I should have shared your grief, but I should have wished you at the same time to trust to your best friends. Goodbye, my daughter, be cheerful; it is necessary to be resigned; keep well, in order to fulfil all your duties. My wife is utterly miserable about your condition; do not increase her sorrow. – Your affectionate father, Napoleon.'*

~ 101 ~

To The Empress, at St. Cloud.

Marienburg, June 3, 1807.

This morning I slept at Marienburg. Yesterday I left Danzig; my health is very good. Every letter that comes from St. Cloud tells me you are always weeping. That is not well; it is necessary for you to keep well and be cheerful.

Hortense is still unwell; what you tell me of her makes me very sorry for her.

Adieu, dear; think of all the affection I bear for you.

Napoleon

~ 102 ~

To The Empress, at St. Cloud.
Finckenstein, June 6, 1807.
My Dear,
I am in flourishing health. Your letter of yesterday pained me; it seems to me that you are always grieving, and that you are not reasonable.

The weather is very fine.

Adieu, dear; I love you and wish to see you cheerful and contented.

Napoleon

~ 103 ~

To The Empress, at St. Cloud.
Friedland, June 15, 1807.
My Dear,
I write you only a line, for I am very tired, by reason of several days' bivouacking. My children have worthily celebrated the anniversary of the battle of Marengo.

The battle of Friedland will be as celebrated by my people, and equally glorious. The entire Russian army routed, 80 cannon captured, 30,000 men taken or slain, 25 Russian generals killed, wounded, or taken, the Russian Guard wiped out.

The battle is worthy of her sisters – Marengo, Austerlitz, Jena. The bulletin will tell you the rest. My loss is not considerable. I out-manoeuvred the enemy successfully.

Be content and without uneasiness.

Adieu, dear; my horse is waiting.

Napoleon

You may give this news as official, if it arrives before the bulletin. They may also fire salvoes. Cambacérès will make the proclamation.

~ 104 ~

To The Empress, at St. Cloud.

Friedland, June 16, 1807, 4 p.m.

My Dear,

Yesterday I despatched Moustache with the news of the battle of Friedland. Since then I have continued to pursue the enemy. Königsberg, which is a town of 80,000 souls, is in my power. I have found there many cannon, large stores, and, lastly, more than 160,000 muskets, which have come from England.

Adieu, dear. My health is perfect, although I have a slight catarrh caused by bivouacking in the rain and cold. Be happy and cheerful.

Yours ever, Napoleon

Friedland. – *On this day he wrote a further letter to the Queen of Holland: 'My daughter, I have your letter dated Orleans. Your grief pains me, but I should like you to possess more courage; to live is to suffer, and the true man is always fighting for mastery over himself. I do not like to see you unjust towards the little Napoleon Louis, and towards all your friends. Your mother and I had hoped to be more to you than we are.' She had been sent to take the waters of Cauterets, and had left her child Napoleon Louis (who died at Forli, 1831) with Josephine, who writes to her daughter (June 11th): 'He amuses me much; he is so gentle. I find he has all the ways of that poor child that we mourn.' And a few days later: 'There remains to you a husband, an interesting child, and a mother whose love you know.'*

~ 105 ~

To The Empress, at St. Cloud.

Tilsit, June 19, 1807.

This morning I despatched Tascher to you, to calm all your fears. Here all goes splendidly. The battle of Friedland has decided everything. The enemy is confounded, overwhelmed, and greatly weakened.

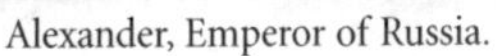
Alexander, Emperor of Russia.

Louise, Queen of Prussia.

My health is good, and my army is superb.

Adieu, dear. Be cheerful and contented.

Napoleon

Tilsit. – *On June 21st an armistice was concluded between France and Russia, shortly followed by a more lasting peace. The two powers effectively divided Europe between them. Alexander of Russia soon began an attack on Sweden and against the Turks whilst Napoleon turned his attention to Spain and Portugal.*

~ 106 ~

To The Empress, at St. Cloud.

Tilsit, June 22, 1807.

My Dear,

I have your letter of June 10th. I am sorry to see you are so depressed. You will see by the bulletin that I have concluded a suspension of arms, and that we are negotiating peace. Be contented and cheerful.

I despatched Borghèse to you, and, twelve hours later, Moustache; therefore you should have received in good time my letters and the news of the grand battle of Friedland.

I am wonderfully well, and wish to hear that you are happy.

Yours ever, Napoleon

~ 107 ~

To The Empress, at St. Cloud.
Tilsit, June 25, 1807.
My Dear,

I have just seen the Emperor Alexander. I was much pleased with him. He is a very handsome, young, and kind-hearted Emperor; he has more intelligence than people usually give him credit for. Tomorrow he will lodge in the town of Tilsit.

Adieu, dear. I am very anxious to hear that you are well and happy. My health is very good.

Napoleon

~ 108 ~

To The Empress, at St. Cloud.
Tilsit, July 3, 1807.
My Dear,

M. de Turenne will give you full details of all that has occurred here. Everything goes excellently. I think I told you that the Emperor of Russia drinks your health with much cordiality. He, as well as the King of Prussia, dines with me every day. I sincerely trust that you are happy.

Adieu, dear. A thousand loving remembrances.

Napoleon

~ 109 ~

To The Empress, at St. Cloud.
Tilsit, July 6, 1807.

I have your letter of June 25th. I was grieved to see that you were selfish, and that the success of my arms should have no charm for you.

The beautiful Queen of Prussia is to come tomorrow to dine with me.

I am well, and am longing to see you again, when destiny shall so order it. Still, it may be sooner than we expect.

Adieu, dear; a thousand loving remembrances.

Napoleon

~ 110 ~

To The Empress, at St. Cloud.
Tilsit, July 7, 1807.
My Dear,

Yesterday the Queen of Prussia dined with me. I had to be on the defence against some further concessions she wished me to make to her husband; but I was very polite, and yet held firmly to my policy. She is very charming. I shall soon give you the details, which I could not possibly give you now unless at great length. When you read this letter, peace with Prussia and Russia will be concluded, and Jerome acknowledged King of Westphalia, with a population of three millions. This news is for yourself alone.

Adieu, dear; I love you, and wish to know that you are cheerful and contented.

~ 111 ~

To The Empress, at St. Cloud.
Tilsit, July 8, 1807.

The Queen of Prussia is really charming; she flirts a lot with me; but don't be jealous; I am a waterproof cloth and all that just slides off. It would cost me too much to play the lover.

Napoleon

July 8. – *Presumed date.*

~ 112 ~

To The Empress, at St. Cloud.

Dresden, July 18, 1807, noon.

My Dear,

Yesterday I arrived at Dresden at 5 p.m., in excellent health, although I remained a hundred hours in the carriage without getting out. I am staying here with the King of Saxony, with whom I am highly pleased. I have now therefore traversed more than half the distance that separates us.

It is very likely that one of these fine nights I may descend upon St. Cloud like a jealous husband, so beware.

Adieu, dear; I shall have great pleasure in seeing you.

Yours ever, Napoleon

~ 113 ~

To The Empress, at Paris.

Milan, November 25, 1807.

My Dear,

I have been here two days. I am very glad that I did not bring you here; you would have suffered dreadfully in crossing Mont Cenis, where a storm detained me twenty-four hours.

I found Eugène in good health; I am very pleased with him. The Princess is ill; I went to see her at Monza. She has had a miscarriage; she is getting better.

Adieu, dear.

Napoleon

Milan. – *Arriving here on the morning of the 22nd, Napoleon goes first to hear the* Te Deum *at the Cathedral, then to see Eugène's wife at the Monza Palace; in the evening to the La Scala Theatre, and finishes the day by working most of the night. He was drawing up plans for the economic blockade of England.*

Mont Cenis. – *Napoleon was overtaken by a storm which put his life in danger. He was fortunate enough to reach a cave in which he took refuge.*

Eugène. – *The Decree of Milan, by which, in default of male and legitimate children of the direct line(the Decree itself says* 'nos enfants et decendants males, legitimes et naturals'*), he adopted Eugène for his son and his successor to the throne of Italy, gave to those who knew the Emperor the proof that he had excluded him from all inheritance in the Imperial Crown of France. This is an important moment for the childless Josephine.*

~ 114 ~

To The Empress, at Paris.

Venice, November 30, 1807.

I have your letter of November 22nd. The last two days I have been at Venice. The weather is very bad, which has not prevented me from sailing over the lagoons in order to see the different forts.

I am glad to see you are enjoying yourself at Paris.

The King of Bavaria, with his family, as well as the Princess Eliza, are here. I am spending December 2nd here, and that past I shall be on my way home, and very glad to see you.

Adieu, dear.

Napoleon

Venice. – *The Venetians gave Napoleon a wonderful welcome and the Viceroy and the Vicereine of Italy, the King and Queen of Bavaria, the Princess of Lucca, the King of Naples (Joseph), the Grand Duke of Berg, the Prince of Neufchâtel, were also present.*

November 30th. – *Leaving Milan, Napoleon came straight through Brescia to Verona, where he dined with the King and Queen of Bavaria.*

December 2nd. – *His Coronation Day.*

~ 115 ~

To The Empress, at Paris.

Udine, December 11, 1807.

My Dear,

I have your letter of December 3rd, from which I note that you were much pleased with the *Jardin des Plantes.* Here I am at the extreme limit of my journey; it is possible I may soon be in Paris, where I shall be very glad to see you again. The weather has not as yet been cold here, but very rainy. I have profited by this good season up to the last moment, for I suppose that at Christmas the winter will at length make itself felt.

Adieu, dear.

Yours ever, Napoleon

Udine. – *He is here on the 12th, and then hastens to meet his brother Lucien at Mantua – the main but secret object of his journey to Italy. Lucien is in disgrace within less than three months of the Mantuan interview, for on March 11, 1808, Napoleon writes to his elder brother Joseph, 'Lucien is misconducting himself at Rome ... and is more Roman than the Pope himself. His conduct has been scandalous; he is my open enemy, and that of France ... I will not permit a Frenchman, and one of my own brothers, to be the first to conspire and act against me with a rabble of priests.'*

I may soon be in Paris. – *After leaving Milan he visits the fortifications at Alessandria, and is met by a torchlight procession at Marengo. Letters for two days (December 27-28th) are dated Turin, although Constant says he did not stop there. Crossing Mont Cenis on December 30th he reaches the Tuileries on the evening of New Year's Day (1808).*

~ 116 ~

To The Empress, at Bordeaux.

Bayonne, April 16, 1808.

I have arrived here in good health, rather tired by a dull journey and a very bad road.

I am very glad you stayed behind, for the houses here are wretched and very small.

I go today into a small house in the country, about a mile from the town.

Adieu, dear. Take care of yourself.

Bayonne is half-way between Paris and Madrid, nearly 600 miles from each. Napoleon arrived here April 15th, and left July 21st, returning with Josephine via Pau, Tarbes, Auch, Montauban, Agen, Bordeaux, Rochefort, Nantes. Everywhere he received a hearty welcome, even in La Vendée. He arrived at Paris August 14th, hearing on August 3rd at Bordeaux of (what he calls) the 'horrible catastrophe' of General Dupont's surrender to the Spanish at Baylen.

~ 117 ~

To The Empress, at Bordeaux.

Bayonne, April 17, 1808.

I have just received yours of April 15th. What you tell me of the owner of the country house pleases me. Go and spend the day there sometimes.

I am sending an order for you to have 20,000 francs per month additional while I am away, counting from the 1st of April.

I am lodged atrociously. I am leaving this place in an hour, to occupy a country-house (*bastide*) about a mile away. The Infant Don Carlos and five or six Spanish grandees are here, the Prince of the Asturias fifty miles away. King Charles and the Queen are due. I don't know how I shall accommodate all these people. Everything here is still so rustic (*a l'auberge*). The health of my troops in Spain is good.

It took me some time to understand your little jokes; I have laughed at your recollections. Oh you women, what memories you have!

My health is fairly good, and I love you most affectionately. I wish you to give my kind regards to everybody at Bordeaux; I have been too busy to send them to anybody.

Napoleon

~ 118 ~

To The Empress, at Bordeaux.

April 21, 1808.

I have just received your letter of April 19th. Yesterday I had the Prince of the Asturias and his suite to dinner, which occasioned me considerable embarrassment. I am waiting for Charles IV and the Queen.

My health is good. I am now sufficiently recovered for the campaign.

Adieu, dear. Your letters always give me much pleasure.

Napoleon

Prince of the Asturias. – *Ferdinand, eldest son of the King of Spain. The Emperor had received him at the château of Marrac, paid him all the honours due to royalty, while evading the word 'Majesty', and insisting the same day on his giving up all claim to the Crown of Spain. Constant says he was heavy of gait, and rarely spoke.*

The Queen. – *A woman of violent passions. The Prince of the Asturias had designs on his mother's life, while the Queen openly begged Napoleon to put the Prince to death. On May 9th Napoleon wrote to Talleyrand to prepare to take charge of Ferdinand at Valençay, adding that if the latter were 'go with some pretty woman, whom we are sure of, all the better for us.'*

~ 119 ~

To The Empress, at Bordeaux.

Bayonne, April 23, 1808.

My Dear,

A son has been born to Hortense; I am highly delighted. I am not surprised that you tell me nothing of it, since your letter is dated the 21st, and the child was only born on the 20th, during the night.

You can start on the 26th, sleep at Mont de Marsan, and arrive here on the 27th. Have your best dinner-service sent on here on the 25th, in the evening. I have made arrangements for you to have a little house in the country, next to the one I have. My health is good.

I am waiting for Charles IV and his wife.

Adieu, dear.

Napoleon

A son has been born. – *Charles Louis Napoleon, later the Emperor Napoleon III. By a plebiscite of the year XII (1804-5) the children of Louis and Hortense were to be the heirs of Napoleon, and in conformity with this the child born on April 20th at 17 Rue Lafitte was inscribed on the register of the Civil List destined for princes of the blood. His two elder brothers had not been so honoured, but in due course the King of Rome was entered thereon. Had Louis accepted the Crown of Spain which Napoleon had in vain offered to him, the chances are that Napoleon would never have divorced Josephine. Louis and Hortense insist that the father's name be preserved by the child, who is called Charles Louis Napoleon, and not Charles Napoleon, which was the Emperor's first choice. In either case the name of the dead firstborn had been preserved.*

Arrive on the 27th. – *Josephine, always wishful to humour her husband's love of punctuality, duly arrived on the day fixed, and took up her abode with her husband in the château of Marrac. Ferdinand wrote to his uncle in Madrid to beware of the* cursed *Frenchmen, telling him also that Josephine had been badly received at Bayonne. The letter was intercepted, and Napoleon wrote to*

Murat that the writer was a liar, a fool, and a hypocrite. The Emperor, in fact, never trusted the Prince henceforward. Bausset, who translated the letter, tells how the Emperor could scarcely believe that the Prince would use so strong an adjective, but was convinced on seeing the word maldittos, *which he remarked was almost the Italian* – maledetto.

~ 120 ~

To The Empress, at St. Cloud.
Erfurt, September 29, 1808.
I have a bit of a cold. I have received your letter, dated Malmaison. I am well pleased with the Emperor and every one here. It is an hour after midnight, and I am tired.

Adieu, dear; take care of yourself.

Napoleon

Leaving St. Cloud on September 22nd, Napoleon is at Metz on the 23rd, at Kaiserlautern on the 24th, where he sends a message to the Empress in a letter to Cambacérès; on the 27th is at Erfurt. On the 28th the Emperors of France and Russia sign a Convention of Alliance. Napoleon leaves Erfurt October 14th (the anniversary of Jena), travels incognito, arriving back at St. Cloud on October 18th.

I have rather a cold. – *Napoleon had insisted on going to explore a new road he had ordered between Metz and Mayence and which no one had dared to say was not complete. The road was so bad that the carriage of the maître des requêtes, who had been summoned to account for the faulty work, fell a hundred feet down a ravine near Kaiserlautern.*

I am pleased with the Emperor and every one here. – *Which included a number of kings. Besides the two Emperors, the King of Prussia was represented by his brother Prince William, Austria by General Vincent, and there were also the Kings of Saxony, Bavaria, Württemberg, Westphalia, and Naples, the Prince Primate (Prince-Archbishop of Mayence, Carl-Theodore von Dalberg), the Princes of Anhalt, Coburg, Saxe-Weimar, Darmstadt, Baden, and Nassau.*

Talleyrand, Champagny, Maret, Duroc, Berthier, and Caulaincourt, with Oudinot, Soult, and Lauriston accompanied Napoleon.

~ 121 ~

To The Empress, at St. Cloud.

October 9, 1808.

My Dear,

I have received your letter. I note with pleasure that you are well. I have just been shooting over the battlefield of Jena. We had breakfast (*déjeuné*) at the spot where I bivouacked on the night of the battle.

I assisted at the Weimar ball. The Emperor Alexander dances; but not I. Forty years are forty years.

My health is really sound, in spite of a few trifling ailments.

Adieu, dear; I hope to see you soon.

Yours ever, Napoleon

Shooting over the battlefield of Jena. – *The presence of the Emperor Alexander on this occasion was considered a great affront to his recent ally, the King of Prussia. The Emperor Alexander, albeit short-sighted, succeeded in killing a stag, at eight feet distance, at the first shot.*

~ 122 ~

To The Empress, at St. Cloud.

My Dear,

I write to you seldom; I am very busy. Conversations which last whole days, and which do not improve my cold. Still all goes well. I am pleased with Alexander; he ought to be on my side. If he were a woman, I think I should make him my sweetheart. I shall be back to you shortly; keep well and let me find you plump and rosy.

Adieu, dear.

Napoleon

I am pleased with Alexander. – *For the time being Josephine also had reason to be pleased with Alexander, who failed to secure his sister's hand for Napoleon.*

He ought to be on my side. – *He might have been, had not Napoleon purposely evaded the Eastern Question. 'Alexander', Napoleon told O'Meara, 'wanted to get Constantinople, which I would not allow, as it would have destroyed the equilibrium of power in Europe. I reflected that France would gain Egypt, Syria, and the islands, which would have been nothing in comparison with what Russia would have obtained. I considered that the barbarians of the north were already too powerful, and probably in the course of time would overwhelm all Europe, as I now think they will. Austria already trembles: Russia and Prussia united, Austria falls, and England cannot prevent it.'*

~ 123 ~

To The Empress, at Paris.

November 3, 1808.

I arrived tonight with considerable trouble. I had ridden several stages at full speed. Still, I am well.

Tomorrow I'm leaving for Spain.

My troops are arriving in force.

Adieu, dear.

Yours ever, Napoleon

I arrived tonight – *at Bayonne on his way to campaign in Spain.*

~ 124 ~

To The Empress, at Paris.

Tolosa, November 5, 1808.

I am at Tolosa. I am leaving for Vittoria, where I shall be in a few hours. I am fairly well, and I hope everything will soon be completed.

Napoleon

~ 125 ~

To The Empress, at Paris.

Vittoria, November 7.

My Dear,

I have been the last two days at Vittoria. I am in good health. My troops are arriving daily; the Guard arrived today.

The King is in very good health. I am very busy.

I know that you are in Paris. Never doubt my affection.

Napoleon

The King. – *Joseph Bonaparte, moved from the throne of Naples to that of Spain.*

~ 126 ~

To The Empress, at Paris.

Burgos, November 14, 1808.

Matters here are progressing at a great rate. The weather is very fine. We are successful. My health is very good.

Napoleon

~ 127 ~

To The Empress, at Paris.

November 26, 1808.

I have received your letter. I trust that your health be as good as mine is, although I am very busy. All goes well here.

I think you should return to the Tuileries on December 21st, and from that date give a concert daily for eight days.

Yours ever, Napoleon

Kind regards to Hortense and to M. Napoleon.

~ 128 ~

To The Empress, at Paris.

December 7, 1808.

Your letter of the 28th to hand. I am glad to see that you are well. You will have seen that young Tascher has distinguished himself, which has pleased me. My health is good.

Here we are enjoying Parisian weather of the last fortnight in May. We are hot, and have no fires; but the nights are rather cool. Madrid is quiet. All my affairs prosper.

Adieu, dear.

Yours ever, Napoleon

Kind regards to Hortense and to M. Napoleon.

Written from the Imperial Camp outside Madrid. Neither Napoleon nor Joseph entered the capital, but King Joseph took up his abode at the Prado, the castle of the Kings of Spain, two miles away; while the Emperor was generally at Chamartin, some five miles distant. He had arrived on the heights surrounding Madrid on his Coronation Day (December 2nd), and does not fail to remind his soldiers and his people of this auspicious coincidence. The bulletin concludes with a tirade against England, whose conduct is 'shameful', but her troops 'well disciplined and superb'. It declares that Spain has been treated by them as they have treated Holland, Sardinia, Austria, Russia, and Sweden. 'They foment war everywhere; they distribute weapons like poison; but they shed their blood only for their direct and personal interests.'

Parisian weather of the last fortnight in May. – *In his bulletin of the 13th, he says: 'Never has such a month of December been known in this country; one would think it the beginning of spring.' But ten days later all was changed. Other letters of this date are headed Madrid.*

~ 129 ~

To The Empress, at Paris.
Chamartin, December 10, 1808.
My Dear,
Your letter to hand, in which you tell me what bad weather you are having in Paris; here it is the best weather imaginable. Please tell me what these alterations Hortense is making mean; I hear she is sending away her servants. Is it because they have refused to do what was required? Give me some particulars. Reforms are not desirable.

Adieu, dear. The weather here is delightful. All goes excellently, and I pray you to keep well.

Napoleon

~ 130 ~

To The Empress, at Paris.
December 21, 1808.
You ought to have been at the Tuileries on the 12th. I trust you may have been pleased with your rooms.

I have authorised the presentation of Kourakin to you and the family; be kind to him, and let him take part in your plays.

Adieu, dear. I am well. The weather is rainy; it is rather cold.

Kourakin. – *Alexander Kourakin was the new Russian Ambassador at Paris, removed thence from Vienna to please Napoleon, and to replace Tolstoy, who, according to Savary, was always quarrelling with French officers on military points. This matter had been arranged at Erfurt. In 1811 Kourakin bore the brunt of Napoleon's anger as the French prepared for war against Russia.*

~ 131 ~

To The Empress, at Paris.

Madrid, December 22, 1808.

I start at once to outmanoeuvre the English, who appear to have received reinforcements and wish to look big.

The weather is fine, my health perfect; don't be uneasy.

Napoleon

English. – *Sir John Moore's expeditionary corps, sent to assist the Spanish revolt against Napoleon.*

~ 132 ~

To The Empress, at Paris.

Benavente, December 31, 1808.

My Dear,

The last few days I have been in pursuit of the English, but they flee panic-stricken. They have coldly abandoned the remnant of La Romana's army in order not to delay their retreat a single half day. More than a hundred waggons of their baggage have already been taken. The weather is very bad.

Lefebvre has been captured. He took part in a skirmish with 300 of his Chasseurs; these idiots crossed a river by swimming and threw themselves in the midst of the English cavalry; they killed several, but on their return Lefebvre had his horse wounded; it was swimming, the current took him to the bank where the English were; he was taken. Console his wife.

Adieu, dear. Bessières, with 10,000 cavalry, is at Astorga.

Napoleon

A happy New Year to everybody.

The English flee panic-stricken. – *The next day Napoleon writes to Fouché to have songs written, and caricatures made of them, which are also to be translated into German and Italian, and circulated in Germany and Italy.*

The weather is very bad. – *Including 18 degrees of frost. Savary says the cold was worse than Poland – and that they ran a risk of being buried in the snow. The Emperor had to march on foot and was very much tired. 'On these occasions', adds Savary, 'the Emperor was not selfish, as people would have us believe ... he shared his supper and his fire with all who accompanied him: he went so far as to make those eat whom he saw in need of it.' Napier gives other details: 'Napoleon, on December 22nd, has 50,000 men at the foot of the Guadarrama. A deep snow choked the passes of the Sierra, and after twelve hours' toil the advanced guards were still on the wrong side: the general commanding reported the road impracticable, but Napoleon, dismounting, placed himself at the head of the column, and amidst storms of hail and driving snow, led his soldiers over the mountain.' At the passage of the Esla Moore escapes Napoleon by twelve hours.*

Lefebvre. – *As they neared Benavente the slush became frightful, and the artillery could not keep pace. General Lefebvre-Desnouettes went forward, with the Chasseurs of the Guard, forded the Esla with four squadrons, was outnumbered by the English (3,000 to 300), but he and sixty of his Chasseurs were captured. He was brought in great triumph to Sir John Moore. He spent the next four years as a prisoner in Cheltenham before escaping back to France in 1812.*

~ 133 ~

To The Empress, at Paris.

January 3, 1809.

My Dear,

I have received your letters of the 18th and 21st. I am close behind the English.

The weather is cold and rigorous, but all goes well.

Adieu, dear.

Yours ever, Napoleon

A happy New Year, and a very happy one, to my Josephine.

Probably written from Astorga, where he arrived on January 1st, having brought 50,000 men two hundred miles in ten days.

Your letters. – *These probably, and others received by a courier, decided him to let Soult follow the English to Corunna. He himself prepares to return, for Fouché and Talleyrand are in league, the slim and slippery Metternich is ambassador at Paris, Austria is arming, and the whole political horizon, apparently bright at Erfurt, completely overcast. Ignoring the complicity of Fouché, the whole weight of his anger falls on Talleyrand, who loses the post of High Chamberlain, which he had enjoyed since 1804: 'You are a thief, a coward, a man without honour; you do not believe in God; you have all your life been a traitor to your duties; you have deceived and betrayed everybody: nothing is sacred to you; you would sell your own father. I have loaded you down with gifts, and there is nothing that you would not undertake against me. Thus, for the past ten months, you have been shameless enough, because you supposed, rightly or wrongly, that my affairs in Spain were going astray, to say to all who would listen to you that you always blamed my plans there, whereas it was yourself who first put it into my head, and who persistently urged it. And that man, that unfortunate (he was thus designating the Duc d'Enghien), by whom was I advised of the place of his residence? Who drove me to deal cruelly with him? What then are you after? What do you want? What do you hope for? Do you dare say? You deserve that I should smash you like a wine-glass. I can do it, but I despise you too much to take the trouble.'*

~ 134 ~

To The Empress, at Paris.

Benavente, January 5, 1809.

My Dear,

I write you a line. The English are in utter rout; I have instructed the Duke of Dalmatia to pursue them closely (*L'épee dans les reins*). I am well; the weather bad.

Adieu, dear.

Napoleon

~ 135 ~

To The Empress, at Paris.
January 8, 1809.
I have received yours of the 23rd and 26th. I am sorry to see you have toothache. I have been here two days. The weather is what we must expect at this season. The English are embarking. I am in good health. Adieu, dear. I am writing to Hortense. Eugène has a daughter.

Yours ever, Napoleon

This letter and the one which follows were written at Valladolid. Here he received a deputation asking that his brother may reside in Madrid, to which he agrees, and awaits its arrangement before setting out for Paris. He leaves Valladolid January 17th, and is in Paris on January 24th. He rode the first seventy miles, to Burgos, in five and a half hours, stopping only to change horses. Well might Savary say, 'Never had a sovereign ridden at such a speed.'

Eugène has a daughter. – *The Princess Eugénie-Hortense, born December 23rd at Milan; married the hereditary Prince of Hohenzollern Hechingen.*

~ 136 ~

To The Empress, at Paris.
January 9, 1809.
Moustache brings me your letter of 31st December. I see from it, dear, that you are sad and have very gloomy thoughts. Austria will not make war on me; if she does, I have 150,000 men in Germany and as many on the Rhine, and 400,000 Germans to reply to her. Russia will not separate herself from me. They are foolish in Paris; all goes well.

I shall be at Paris the moment I think it worth while. I advise you to beware of ghosts; one fine day, at two o'clock in the morning.

But adieu, dear; I am well, and am yours ever,

Napoleon

They are foolish in Paris. – *If not worse. Talleyrand, Fouché, and others were forming what amounted to a conspiracy, and the Empress herself, wittingly or unwittingly, had served as their tool. For the first time she answers a deputation of the* Corps Législatif, *who come to congratulate her on her husband's victories, and says that doubtless his Majesty would be very sensible of the homage of an assembly* which represents the nation. *Napoleon sees in this remark a germ of aggression on behalf of his parliament, more especially when emphasised by 125 votes against a Government Bill. He takes the effective but somewhat severe step of contradicting his wife in the* Moniteur, *or rather declaring that the Empress knew the laws too well not to know that the Emperor was the chief representative of the People, then the Senate, and last the* Corps Législatif. *'It would be a wild and even criminal assertion to try to represent the nation before the Emperor.'*

All through the first half of 1809 another dangerous plot, of which the centre was the Princess of Tour and Taxis, had its threads far and wide. It stirs up strife between the Emperor and Soult, by suggesting that the latter should be made King of Portugal.

~ 137 ~

To the Empress, at Strasburg.

Donauwerth, April 17, 1809.

I arrived here yesterday at 4 a.m.; I am just leaving it. Everything is under way. Military operations are in full swing. Up to the present, there is nothing new. My health is good.

Yours ever, Napoleon

The dangers surrounding Napoleon were immense. The Austrian army, 320,000 strong (with her Landwehr, 544,000 men) and 800 cannon, had never been so great, never so ready for war. The Archduke Ferdinand invaded the Duchy of Warsaw, and had he taken Thorn with its park of 100 cannon, Prussia was to join Austria. England had an army of 40,000 men ready to embark in any direction – to Holland, Belgium, Naples, or Biscay, while conspiracies were afoot to win over the French troops in Portugal who would then receive Moreau as their leader, and march with the Spaniards and English for the Pyrenees. At Paris Talleyrand was in partial disgrace, but he and Fouché were still plotting – the latter, says Pelet, forwarding daily a copy of the private bulletin (prepared for Napoleon's eye alone) to the Bourbons. After Essling and the breaking of the Danube bridge, he hesitated between seizing supreme power himself or offering it to Bernadotte.

On April 8th the Austrians marched into Bavarian territory, and during his supreme command for the next five days Berthier endangered the safety of the French empire in spite of the most elaborate and lucid instructions from Napoleon, which he failed to comprehend. The arrival of Napoleon changed in a moment the position of affairs. Within five days the Austrians were four times defeated, and Ratisbon is once more in the hands of France and her allies. A few days later the Archduke Charles writes a letter to Napoleon, which is a fair type of those charming yet stately manners which made him at that moment the most popular man in Europe. 'Sire', he writes, 'your Majesty's arrival was announced to me by the thunder of artillery, without giving me time to compliment you thereon. Scarcely advised of your presence, I was made sensible of it by the losses which you have caused me. You have taken many of my men, Sire; my troops also have made some thousands of prisoners in places where you did not direct the operations. I propose to your Majesty to exchange them man for man, rank for rank, and if that offer is agreeable to you, please let me know your intentions for the place destined for the exchange. I feel flattered, sire, in fighting against the greatest captain of the age. I should be more happy if destiny had chosen me to procure for my country the benefit of a lasting peace. Whichsoever they be, the events of war or the approach of peace, I beg your Majesty to believe that my desires always carry me to meet you, and that I hold myself equally honoured in finding the sword, or the olive branch, in the hand of your Majesty.'

Donauwerth. – *On the same day Napoleon writes almost an identical letter to Cambacérès, adding, however, the news that the Tyrolese are in full revolt.*

On April 24th is issued from Ratisbon his proclamation to the army: –

'Soldiers, you have justified my expectations. You have made up for your number by your bravery. You have gloriously marked the difference between the soldiers of Caesar and the armed cohorts of Xerxes. In a few days we have triumphed in the pitched battles of Thann, Abensberg, and Eckmühl, and in the combats of Peising, Landshut, and Ratisbon. A hundred cannon, forty flags, fifty thousand prisoners ... Before a month we shall be at Vienna.'

~ 138 ~

To the Empress, at Strasburg.

Enns, May 6, 1809, noon.

My Dear,

I have received your letter. The ball that touched me has not wounded me; it barely grazed the Achilles tendon.

My health is very good. You are wrong to be uneasy.

My affairs here go excellently.

Yours ever, Napoleon

Kind regards to Hortense and the Duke of Berg.

May 6th. – *On May 1st Napoleon was still at Braunau, waiting for news from Davout. Travelling by night at his usual speed he reached Lambach at noon on May 2nd, and Wels on the 3rd. The next morning he heard Massena's cannon at Ebersberg, but reaches the field at nightfall – too late to save the heavy cost of Massena's frontal attack. The French lost at least 1,500 killed and wounded; the Austrians (under Hiller) the same number killed and 7,000 prisoners. Pelet defends Massena, and quotes the bulletin of May 4th (omitted from the* Correspondence*): 'It is one of the finest feats of arms of which history can preserve the memory! The traveller will stop and say, "It is here, it is here, in these superb positions, that an army of 35,000 Austrians was routed by two French divisions" (Pelet ii. 225).*

Between April 17th and May 6th there is no letter to Josephine preserved, but plenty to Eugène, and all severe – not so much for incapacity as for not keeping the Emperor advised of what was really happening. On May 6th he had received no news for over a week.

The ball that touched me. – *i.e. at Ratisbon. This was the second time Napoleon had been wounded in battle – the first time by an English bayonet at Toulon. On the present occasion (April 23rd) Méneval seems to be the best authority: 'Napoleon was seated on a spot from which he could see the attack on the town of Ratisbon. He was beating the ground with his riding-whip, when a bullet, supposed to have been fired from a Tyrolean carbine, struck him on the big toe (Marbot says 'right ankle', which is correct). The news of his wound spread rapidly from file to file, and he was forced to mount on horseback to show himself to his troops. Although his boot had not been cut the contusion was a very painful one' and in the first house he went to for a moment's rest, he fainted.*

Duke of Berg. – *Napoleon Louis, Prince Royal of Holland, and Grand Duke of Berg from March 3, 1809.*

~ 139 ~

To the Empress, at Strasburg.

Saint-Polten, May 9, 1809.

My Dear,

I write to you from Saint-Polten. Tomorrow I shall be before Vienna; it will be exactly a month to the day after the Austrians crossed the Inn, and violated peace.

My health is good, the weather splendid, and the soldiery very cheerful; there is wine here.

Keep well.

Yours ever, Napoleon

Almost an exact duplicate of this letter goes on to Paris to Cambacérès, as also of the letter which follows. The moment the Emperor had heard that the Archduke had left Budweiss and was going by the circuitous route via Krems to Vienna, he left Enns (May 7th) and reached Moelk the same evening. The next day he started for Saint-Polten (already evacuated by Hiller). On his way he saw the ruins of Dirnstein Castle, where Richard Coeur de Lion had been imprisoned.

~ **140** ~

To The Empress, at Strasburg.

Schönbrunn, May 12, 1809.

I am despatching the brother of the Duchess of Montebello to let you know that I am master of Vienna, and that everything here goes perfectly. My health is very good.

Napoleon

Schönbrunn. – *situated a mile from Vienna, across the little river of that name. The Emperor drank a glassful from the beautiful spring, Schön Brunn, every morning. Napoleon found the people of Vienna less favourable to the French than in 1805; and Count Rapp told him 'the people were everywhere tired of us and of our victories. He did not like these sorts of reflections.'*

May 12th. – *On May 13th is dated the* seventh *bulletin of the army of Germany, but none of the Bulletins 2 to 6 are in the* Correspondence. *It states that on the 10th Napoleon is before Vienna; the Archduke Maximilian refuses to surrender; on the 11th, at 9 p.m., the bombardment commences, and by daybreak the city capitulated, and the Archduke fled. In his proclamation Napoleon blamed him and the house of Austria for the bombardment. 'While fleeing from the city, their adieux to the inhabitants have been murder and arson; like Medea, they have with their own hands slain their children.'*

~ **141** ~

To the Empress, at Strasburg.

Ebersdorf, May 27, 1809.

I am despatching a page to tell you that Eugène has rejoined me with all his army; that he has perfectly performed the task that I entrusted him with; and has almost entirely destroyed the enemy's army opposed to him.

I send you my proclamation to the army of Italy, which will make you understand all this.

I am very well.

Yours ever, Napoleon

P.S. You can have this proclamation printed at Strasburg, and have it translated into French and German, in order that it may be scattered and broadcast over Germany. Give a copy of the proclamation to the servant who goes on to Paris.

Ebersdorf. – *Written five days after the murderous battle of Essling. As Napoleon said in his tenth bulletin, 'The passage of a river like the Danube, in front of an enemy knowing perfectly the localities, and having the inhabitants on its side, is one of the greatest operations of war which it is possible to conceive.' The Danube hereabouts is a thousand yards wide, and thirty feet deep. But the rising of its water fourteen feet in three days was what no one had expected. At Ebersdorf the first branch of the Danube was 500 yards across to an islet, thence 340 yards across the main current to Lobau, the vast island three miles broad and nearly three miles long, separated from the farther bank by another 150 yards of Danube. Bertrand had made excellent bridges, but on the 22nd the main one was carried away by a barge.*

Eugène ... has completely performed the task. – *At the commencement of the campaign the Viceroy was taken unprepared in Italy. The Archduke John, exactly his own age (twenty-seven), was burning with hatred of France. Eugène had the impudence, with far inferior forces, to attack him at Sacile on April 16th, but was repulsed with a loss (including prisoners) of 6,000 men. It is now necessary to retire, and the Archduke follows him leisurely, almost within sight of Verona. By the end of April the news of Eckmühl has reached both armies, and by May 1st the Austrians are in full retreat. As usual, Napoleon has already divined their altered plan of campaign, and writes from Braunau on this very day, 'I doubt not that the enemy may have retired before you; it is necessary to pursue him with activity, whilst coming to join me as soon as possible via*

Carinthia. The junction with my army will probably take place beyond Bruck. It is probable I shall be at Vienna by the 10th to the 15th of May.' It is the successful performance of this task of joining him and of driving back the enemy to which Napoleon alludes in the letter. The Viceroy had been reproved for fighting at Sacile without his cavalry, for his precipitous retreat on Verona; and only two days earlier the Emperor had told him that if affairs went worse he was to send for the King of Naples (Murat) to take command. 'I am no longer grieved at the blunders you have committed, but because you do not write to me, and give me no chance of advising you, and even of regulating my own affairs here conformably.' On May 8th Eugène defeats the Austrians on the Piave, and the Archduke John loses nearly 10,000 men and 15 cannon. Harassed in their retreat, they regain their own territory on May 14th – the day after the capitulation of Vienna. From now on Eugène with part of the army, and Macdonald with the rest, force their way past all difficulties, so that when the junction with the Grand Army occurs at Bruck, Napoleon sends (May 27th) the following proclamation: 'Soldiers of the army of Italy, you have gloriously attained the goal that I marked out for you ... Surprised by a perfidious enemy before your columns were united, you had to retreat to the Adige. But when you received the order to advance, you were on the memorable fields of Arcola, and there you swore on the spirits of our fallen heroes to triumph. You have kept your word at the battle of the Piave, at the combats of San-Daniel, Tarvis, and Goritz; you have taken by assault the forts of Malborghetto, of Prediel, and made the enemy's divisions, entrenched in Prewald and Laybach, surrender. You had not then passed the Drave, and already 25,000 prisoners, 60 cannon, and 10 flags signal your valour.' This is the proclamation alluded to in this letter to Josephine.

~ 142 ~

To the Empress, at Strasburg.

Ebersdorf; May 29, 1809, 7 p.m.

My Dear,

I have been here since yesterday; I am stopped by the river. The bridge has been burnt; I shall cross at midnight. Everything here goes as I wish it, i.e., very well.

The Austrians have been struck down (*frappé de la foudre*).

Adieu, dear.

Yours ever, Napoleon

May 29th. – *The date is wrong; it should be May 19th or 24th, probably the latter. It sets at rest the vexed question how the Danube bridge was broken, and seems to confirm Marbot's version of a floating barge on fire, purposely sent down by an Austrian officer of Jägers, who won the rare order of Maria Theresa for performing more than his duty. Bertrand gained his Emperor's lifelong admiration by his expedients at this time. Everything had to be utilised – anchors for the boat bridges were made by filling fishermen's baskets with bullets; and a naval contingent of 1,200 sailors from Antwerp proved invaluable.*

~ 143 ~

To the Empress, at Strasburg.

Ebersdorf; May 31, 1809.

Your letter of the 26th to hand. I have written you that you can go to Plombières. I do not care for you to go to Baden; it is not necessary to leave France. I have ordered the two princes to re-enter France.

The loss of the Duke of Montebello, who died this morning, has grieved me exceedingly. Thus everything ends!!

Adieu, dear; if you can help to console the poor marshal's wife, do so.

Yours ever, Napoleon

I have ordered the two princes to re-enter France. – *After so critical a battle as the battle of Essling the Emperor's first thoughts were concerning his succession – had he been killed or captured. He was therefore seriously annoyed that the heir apparent and his younger brother had both been taken out of the country without his permission. He therefore writes to the Queen of Holland on*

May 28th from Ebersdorf: 'My daughter, I am seriously annoyed that you have left France without my permission, and especially that you have taken my nephews out of it. Since you are at Baden stay there, but an hour after receiving the present letter send my two nephews back to Strasburg to be near the Empress – they ought never to go out of France. It is the first time I have had reason to be annoyed with you, but you should not dispose of my nephews without my permission, you should realise what a bad effect it will have. Since the waters at Baden are doing you good you can stay there a few days, but, I repeat, lose not a moment in sending my nephews back to Strasburg. If the Empress is going to the waters at Plombières they may accompany her there, but they must never pass the bridge of Strasburg. – Your affectionate father, Napoleon.' This letter passed through the hands of Josephine at Strasburg, who was so unhappy at not having heard from her husband that she opened it, and writes to Hortense on June 1st when forwarding the letter: 'I advise you to write to him immediately that you have anticipated his intentions, and that your children are with me: that you have only had them a few days in order to see them, and to give them a change of air. The page who is announced in Méneval's letter has not yet arrived. I hope he will bring me a letter from the Emperor, and that at least he will not be as cross with me for your being at Baden. Your children have arrived in excellent health.'

The Duke of Montebello. – *Marshal Lannes died of his wounds. The same day he writes to the Marshal's widow as follows:* 'Ma Cousine, *the Marshal died this morning of the wounds that he received on the field of honour. My sorrow equals yours. I lose the most distinguished general in my whole army, my comrade-in-arms for sixteen years, he whom I looked upon as my best friend. His family and children will always have a special claim on my protection. It is to give you this assurance that I wished to write you this letter, for I feel that nothing can alleviate the righteous sorrow that you will experience.'*

Thus everything ends. – *The fourteenth bulletin says that the end was caused by a pernicious fever, and in spite of Dr. Franck, one of the best physicians in Europe. 'Thus ends one of the most distinguished soldiers France ever possessed.' He had received thirteen wounds. The death of Lannes, and the whole of the Essling period, is best told by Marbot. The loss of Lannes was a more serious one to Napoleon than the whole 20,000 men lost in this battle. The Emperor himself has told us that 'in war men are nothing, a man is everything.'*

~ 144 ~

To the Empress, at Strasburg.
Schönbrunn, June 9, 1809.
I have received your letter; I see with pleasure that you are going to the waters at Plombières, they will do you good.

Eugène is in Hungary with his army. I am well, the weather very fine. I note with pleasure that Hortense and the Duke of Berg are in France.

Adieu, dear.

Yours ever, Napoleon

~ 145 ~

To The Empress, at Plombières.
Schönbrunn, June 16, 1809.
I despatch a page to tell you that, on the 14th, the anniversary of Marengo, Eugène won a battle against the Archduke John and the Archduke Palatine, at Raab, in Hungary; that he has taken 3,000 men, many cannon, 4 flags, and pursued them a long way on the road to Budapest.

Napoleon

Eugène won a battle. – *The remnant of the Archduke John's army, together with Hungarian levies, in all 31,000 men, hold the entrenched camp and banks of the Raab. Eugène defeats it, causing 6,000 casualties, of whom 3,700 were prisoners. Napoleon, in commemoration of the anniversary of Marengo (and Friedland) calls it the little granddaughter of Marengo.*

~ 146 ~

To The Empress, at Plombières.

Schönbrunn, June 19, 1809, noon.

I have your letter, which tells me of your departure for Plombières. I am glad you are making this journey, because I trust it may do you good.

Eugène is in Hungary, and is well. My health is very good, and the army fighting fit.

I am very glad to know that the Grand Duke of Berg is with you.

Adieu, dear. You know my affection for my Josephine; it never varies.

Yours ever, Napoleon

~ 147 ~

To The Empress, at Plombières.

Ebersdorf; July 7, 1809, 5 a.m.

I am despatching a page to bring you the good tidings of the victory of Enzersdorf, which I won on the 5th, and that of Wagram, which I won on the 6th.

The enemy's army flies in disorder, and all goes according to my wishes (*voeux*).

Eugène is well. Prince Aldobrandini is wounded, but slightly. Bessières has been shot through the fleshy part of his thigh; the wound is very slight. Lasalle was killed. My losses are very heavy, but the victory is decisive and complete. We have taken more than 100 cannon, 12 flags, many prisoners. I am sunburnt.

Adieu, dear. I send you a kiss. Kind regards to Hortense.

Napoleon

Wagram. – This *was a massive battle in which both sides suffered heavy losses but at which the Austrians were beaten. Macdonald would be rewarded by Napoleon for punching a hole through the Austrian centre.*

Lasalle. – *A firm favourite of Napoleon, for his sure eye and active bearing. His capture of Stettin with two regiments of hussars was specially noteworthy. Marbot tells a story of how Napoleon gave him 200,000 francs to get married with. A week later the Emperor asked, 'When is the wedding?' 'As soon as I have got some money for it, sire.' 'Why, I gave you 200,000 francs for it last week! What have you done with them?' 'Paid my debts with half, and lost the other half at cards.' Such an admission would have ruined any other general. The Emperor laughed, and merely giving a sharp tug at Lasalle's moustache, ordered Duroc to give him another 200,000.*

I am sunburnt. – *And, as he writes to Cambacérès the same day, tired out, having been sixty out of the previous seventy-two hours in the saddle.*

~ 148 ~

To The Empress, at Plombières.

Wolkersdorf, July 9, 1809, 2 a.m.

My Dear,

All goes here as I wish. My enemies are defeated, beaten, utterly routed. They were in great numbers; I have wiped them out. Today my health is good; yesterday I was rather ill with a surfeit of bile, occasioned by so many hardships, but it has done me much good.

Adieu, dear. I am in excellent health

Napoleon

Wolkersdorf. – *On July 8th he writes to General Clarke that: 'I have the headquarters lately occupied by the craven Francis II, who contented himself with watching the whole affair from the top of a tower, ten miles from the scene of battle.' On this day also he dictated his twenty-fifth bulletin: 'Such is the recital of the battle of Wagram, a decisive and ever illustrious battle, where three to four hundred thousand men, twelve to fifteen hundred guns, fought for great stakes on a field of battle, studied, meditated on, and fortified by the enemy for many months.'*

A surfeit of bile. – *His usual source of relief after extra work or worry. In this case both. Bernadotte had behaved so badly at Wagram, that Napoleon sent him to Paris with the stern rebuke 'A bungler like you is no good to me'. But as usual his anger against an old comrade is short-lived, and he gives General Clarke permission to send Bernadotte to command at Antwerp against an English expeditionary force.*

~ **149** ~

To The Empress, at Plombières.
In the Camp, before Znaim, July 13, 1809.
I send you the armistice concluded yesterday with the Austrian General. Eugène is in Hungary still, and is well. Send a copy of the armistice to Cambacérès, in case he has not yet received one.

I send you a kiss, and am very well.

Napoleon

You may cause this armistice to be printed at Nancy.

~ **150** ~

To The Empress, at Plombières.
Schönbrunn, July 17, 1809.
My Dear,
I have sent you one of my pages. You will have learnt the result of the battle of Wagram, and, later, of the armistice of Znaim.

My health is good. Eugène is well, and I long to know that you, as well as Hortense, are the same.

Give a kiss from me to Monsieur, the Grand Duke of Berg.

Napoleon

~ **151** ~

To The Empress, at Plombières.
Schönbrunn, July 24, 1809.
I have just received yours of July 18th. I note with pleasure that the

waters are doing you good. I see no objection to you going back to Malmaison after you have finished your treatment.

It is hot enough here in all conscience. My health is excellent.

Adieu, dear. Eugène is at Vienna, in the best of health.

Yours ever, Napoleon

~ 152 ~

To The Empress, at Plombières.

Schönbrunn, August 7, 1809.

I see from your letter that you are at Plombières, and intend to stay there. You do well; the waters and the fine climate can only do you good.

I remain here. My health and my affairs follow my wishes.

Please give my kind regards to Hortense and the Napoleons.

Yours ever, Napoleon

My affairs follow my wishes. – *In Austria, possibly, but not elsewhere. Prussia was seething with conspiracy, Russia with ill-concealed hatred, the English had just landed in the Netherlands, and Wellesley had just won Talavera in Spain, beating King Joseph. Soult was apparently no longer trustworthy, Bernadotte a conceited boaster, who had to be publicly snubbed. Clarke and Cambacérès are so slow that Napoleon writes to them (August 10th) 'not to let the English come and surprise you in bed'. Fouché shows more energy than every one else put together, calls out National Guards, and sends them off to meet the northern invasion. The Minister of the Interior, M. Cretet, had just died, and the Emperor had wisely put Fouché, the most competent man available, into his place for the time being.*

~ 153 ~

To The Empress, at Paris.

Schönbrunn, August 21, 1809.

I have received your letter of August 14th, from Plombières; I see from it that by the 18th you will be either at Paris or Malmaison. The heat, which is very great here, will have upset you. Malmaison must be very dry and parched at this time of year.

My health is good. The heat, however, has brought on a slight catarrh.

Adieu, dear.

Napoleon

~ 154 ~

To The Empress, at Malmaison.

Schönbrunn, August 26, 1809.

I have your letter from Malmaison. They bring me word that you are plump, florid, and in the best of health. I assure you Vienna is not an amusing city. I would very much rather be back again in Paris.

Adieu, dear. Twice a week I listen to the comedians (*bouffons*); they are only average; it, however, passes the evenings. There are fifty or sixty women of Vienna, but outsiders (*au parterre*), not having been presented.

Napoleon

~ 155 ~

To The Empress, at Malmaison.

Schönbrunn, August 31, 1809.

I have had no letter from you for several days; the pleasures of Malmaison, the beautiful greenhouses, the beautiful gardens, cause the absent to be forgotten. It is, they say, the rule of your sex. Every one speaks only of your good health; all this is very suspicious.

Tomorrow I am off with Eugène for two days in Hungary. My health is fairly good.

Adieu, dear.

Yours ever, Napoleon

All this is very suspicious. – *Josephine should have been suspicious. Madame*

Walewska had been more than a month at Schönbrunn and on May 4th, 1810, Napoleon has a second son born. He was named Alexander.

~ 156 ~

To The Empress, at Malmaison.

Krems, September 9, 1809.

My Dear,

I arrived here yesterday at 2 a.m.; I have come here to see my troops. My health has never been better. I know that you are very well.

I shall be in Paris at a moment when nobody will expect me. Everything here goes excellently and to my satisfaction.

Adieu, dear.

Napoleon

Krems. – *He left here to review Davout's corps on the field of Austerlitz.*

My health has never been better. – *In his letter to Cambacérès of the same date he writes: 'They have spread in Paris the rumour that I was ill, I know not why; I was never better.' The reason of the rumour was that Corvisart had been sent for to Vienna, as there had been an outbreak of dysentery among the troops.*

~ 157 ~

To The Empress, at Malmaison.

Schönbrunn, September 23, 1809.

I have received your letter of the 16th, and note that you are well. The old maid's house is only worth 120,000 francs; they will never get more for it. Still, I leave you mistress to do what you like, since it amuses you; only, once purchased, don't pull it down to put a rockery there.

Adieu, dear.

Napoleon

The old maid's house. – *Boispreau, belonging to Mademoiselle Julien.*

~ 158 ~

To The Empress, at Malmaison.

Schönbrunn, September 25, 1809.

I have received your letter. Be careful, and I advise you to be vigilant, for one of these nights you will hear a loud knocking.

My health is good. I know nothing about the rumours; I have never been better for many a long year. Corvisart was no use to me.

Adieu, dear; everything here prospers.

Yours ever, Napoleon

~ 159 ~

To The Empress, at Malmaison.

Schönbrunn, October 14, 1809.

My Dear,

I write to advise you that Peace was signed two hours ago by Champagny and Prince Metternich.

Adieu, dear.

Napoleon

October 14th. – *Two days before, Stapps, the young* Tugendbundist *and an admirer of Joan of Arc, had attempted to assassinate Napoleon on parade with a carving knife. The Emperor's letter to Fouché of the 12th October gives the most succinct account:*

'A youth of seventeen, son of a Lutheran minister of Erfurt, sought to approach me on parade today. He was arrested by the officers, and as the little man's agitation had been noticed, suspicion was aroused; he was searched, and a dagger found upon him. I had him brought before me, and the little wretch, who seemed to me fairly well educated, told me that he wished to assassinate me to deliver Austria from the presence of the French. I could distinguish in him neither religious nor political fanaticism. He did not appear to know exactly who or what Brutus was. The fever of excitement he was in prevented our knowing

The knife Stapps used during his attempt to assassinate Napoleon.

more. He will be examined when he has cooled down and fasted. It is possible that it will come to nothing. He will be tried before a military commission.

I wished to inform you of this circumstance in order that it may not be made out more important than it appears to be. I hope it will not leak out; if it does, we shall have to represent the fellow as a madman. If it is not spoken of at all, keep it to yourself. The whole affair made no disturbance at the parade; I myself saw nothing of it.

P.S. – I repeat once more, and you understand clearly, that there is to be no discussion of this occurrence.'

Count Rapp saved the Emperor's life on this occasion, and he, Savary, and Constant, all give detailed accounts. Their narratives are a remarkable object-lesson of the carelessness of the average contemporary spectator in recording dates. Savary gives vaguely the end of September, Constant October 13th, and Count Rapp October 23rd.

~ 160 ~

To The Empress, at Malmaison.

Nymphenburg, near Munich, October 21, 1809.

I arrived here yesterday in the best of health, but shall not start till tomorrow. I shall spend a day at Stuttgart. You will be advised twenty-four hours in advance of my arrival at Fontainebleau.

I look forward with pleasure to seeing you again, and I await that moment impatiently.

I send you a kiss.

Yours ever, Napoleon

Stuttgart. – *General Rapp describes this journey as follows: 'Peace was ratified. We left Nymphenburg and arrived at Stuttgart. Napoleon was received in a style of magnificence, and was lodged in the palace together with his suite. The King was laying out a spacious garden, and men who had been condemned to the galleys were employed to labour in it. The Emperor asked the King who the men were who worked in chains; he replied that they were for the most part rebels who had been taken in his new possessions.*

We set out on the following day. On the way Napoleon alluded to the unfortunate wretches whom he had seen at Stuttgart. "The King of Wurttemberg", said he, "is a very harsh man; but he is very faithful. Of all the sovereigns in Europe he possesses the greatest share of understanding."

We stopped for an hour at Rastadt, where the Princess of Baden and Princess Stephanie had arrived for the purpose of paying their respects to the Emperor. The Grand Duke and Duchess accompanied him as far as Strasburg. On his arrival in that city he received despatches which again excited his displeasure against the Faubourg St. Germain. We proceeded to Fontainebleau; no preparations had been made for the Emperor's reception; there was not even a guard on duty.'

This was on October 26th, at 10 a.m.

~ 161 ~

To The Empress, at Malmaison.

Munich, October 22, 1809.

My Dear,

I start in an hour. I shall be at Fontainebleau from the 26th to 27th; you may meet me there with some of your ladies.

Napoleon

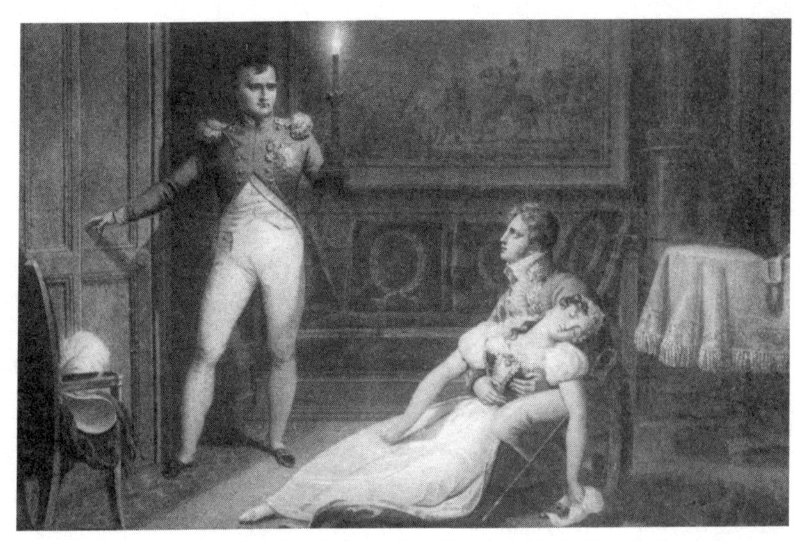

The dramatic scene as Napoleon informs Josephine about his decision to divorce her.

~ 162 ~

To The Empress, at Malmaison.

December 1809, 8 p.m.

My Dear,

I found you today weaker than you ought to be. You have shown courage; it is necessary that you should maintain it and not give way to a doleful melancholy. You must be contented and take special care of your health, which is so precious to me.

If you are attached to me and if you love me, you should show strength of mind and force yourself to be happy. You cannot question my constant and tender friendship, and you would know very imperfectly all the affection I have for you if you imagined that I can be happy if you are unhappy, and contented if you are ill at ease.

Adieu, dear. Sleep well; dream that I wish it.

Napoleon

According to the Correspondence of Napoleon I, *No. 16,058, the date of this letter is December 17th. It seems, however, possible that it is the letter written immediately after his arrival at Trianon, referred to by Méneval, who was, in fact, responsible for it. Thiers, working from the memoirs of Hortense and Cambacérès, gives a most interesting account of the family council, held at 9 p.m. on Friday, December 15th, at the Tuileries. Constant also describes the scene, but gives the Empress credit for showing the most self-command of those chiefly interested. The next day, 11 a.m., Count Lacépède introduced the resolutions of the family council to the Senatus-Consultus. The Decrees of the Committee of the Senate were: '(1) The marriage contracted between the Emperor Napoleon and the Empress Josephine is dissolved. (2) The Empress Josephine will retain the titles and rank of a crowned Empress-Queen. (3) Her jointure is fixed at an annual revenue of £80,000 from the public treasury. (4) Every provision which may be made by the Emperor in favour of the Empress Josephine, out of the funds of the Civil List, shall be obligatory on his successors.' Clause (2) gives considerable trouble to those in charge of imperial protocol. They couldn't find a precedent whether, if they were to meet, Josephine or Marie Louise would take precedence of the other. In addition to the jointure in clause (3), Napoleon gives her £40,000 a year from his privy purse, but kept most of it back for the first two years to pay her 120 creditors.*

They added separate addresses to the Emperor and Empress, the one to the latter seems worthy of quotation: 'Your Imperial and Royal Majesty is about to make for France the greatest of sacrifices; history will preserve the memory of it for ever. The august spouse of the greatest of monarchs cannot be united to his immortal glory by more heroic devotion. For long, Madame, the French people has revered your virtues; it holds dear that loving kindness which inspires your every word, as it directs your every action; it will admire your sublime devotion; it will award for ever to your Majesty, Empress and Queen, the homage of gratitude, respect, and love.'

From a letter of Eugène's to his wife, quoted by Aubenas, it appears that he, with his mother, arrived at Malmaison on Saturday evening, December 16th, (which agrees with Madame d'Avrillon, who says they left the Tuileries at 2.30; Meneval says Napoleon left for Trianon a few hours later whilst Savary writes erroneously that they left the following morning) and that it never ceased raining all the next day, which added to the general depression. On the evening of the 16th Napoleon was at Trianon, writing letters, and we cannot think that if the Emperor had been to Malmaison on the Sunday, Eugène would have included this without comment in the 'some visits' they had received. The Emperor, as we see from the next letter, paid Josephine a visit on the Monday.

~ 163 ~

To The Empress, at Malmaison.

Tuesday, 6 o'clock.

The Queen of Naples, whom I saw at the hunt in the Bois de Boulogne, where I rode down a stag, told me that she left you yesterday at 1 p.m. in the best of health.

Please tell me what you are doing today. As for me, I am very well. Yesterday, when I saw you, I was ill. I expect you will have been out for a drive.

Adieu, dear.

Napoleon

The date of this is Tuesday, December 19th, while the next is Wednesday the 20th.

Queen of Naples. – *For some reason Napoleon had not wanted this sister at Paris this winter, and had written her to this effect from Schönbrunn on October 15th. 'If you were not so far off, and the season so advanced, I would have asked Murat to spend two months in Paris. But you cannot be there before December, which is a horrible season, especially for a Neapolitan.'* (Correspondence of Napoleon I, *No. 15,952) But sister Caroline was not easy to lead; and her husband had in consequence to bear the full weight of the Emperor's displeasure. Murat's finances were in disorder, and Napoleon wrote to Champagny on December 30th to tell Murat plainly that if the borrowed money was not returned to France, it would be taken by force.*

The hunt. – *In pouring rain, in the forest of St. Germain.*

~ 164 ~

To The Empress, at Malmaison.

Trianon, 7 p.m.

My Dear,

I have just received your letter. Savary tells me that you are always crying; that is not well. I trust that you have been out on a drive today. I sent you my quarry. I shall come to see you when you tell me you are reasonable, and that your courage has the upper hand.

Tomorrow, the whole day, I am receiving Ministers.

Adieu, dear. I also am sad today; I need to know that you are satisfied and to learn that your equilibrium (*aplomb*) is restored.

Sleep well.

Napoleon

~ 165 ~

To The Empress, at Malmaison.

Thursday, noon, 1809.

My Dear,

I wished to come and see you today, but I was very busy and rather unwell. Still, I am just off to the Council. Please tell me how you are. This weather is very damp, and not at all healthy.

Napoleon

Thursday, December 21st, is the date.

The weather is very damp. – *Making Malmaison as unhealthy as its very name warranted, and rendering more difficult the task which Madame de Rémusat had set herself of resting Josephine mentally by tiring her physically. This toady had arrived at Malmaison on December 18th. She writes on the*

Friday (December 22nd) beseeching her husband to advise the Emperor to moderate the tone of his letters, especially this one (Thursday, December 21st), which had upset Josephine frightfully. Surely a more harmless letter was never penned. But it is the Rémusat all over; she lives in a chronic atmosphere of suspicion that all her letters are read by the Emperor.

~ 166 ~

To The Empress, at Malmaison.

Trianon.

I should have come to see you today if I had not been obliged to come to see the King of Bavaria, who has just arrived in Paris. I shall come to see you tonight at eight o'clock, and return at ten.

I hope to see you tomorrow, and to see you cheerful and calm.

Adieu, dear.

Napoleon

Date probably Sunday, December 24th.

King of Bavaria. – *Eugène had gone to Meaux to meet his father-in-law.*

~ 167 ~

To The Empress, at Malmaison.

Trianon, Tuesday.

My Dear,

I lay down after you left me yesterday; I am going to Paris. I wish to hear that you are cheerful. I shall come to see you during the week. I have received your letters, which I am going to read in the carriage.

Napoleon

Josephine had gone by special invitation to dine at the little Trianon with Napoleon on Christmas Day, and Madame d'Avrillon says she had a very happy day there. 'On her return she told me how kind the Emperor had been to her, that he had kept her all the evening, saying the kindest things to her.' Eugène, moreover, confirms Madame d'Avrillon in his letter to his wife of December 26th: 'My dear Auguste, the Emperor came on Sunday to see the Empress. Yesterday she went to Trianon to see him, and stayed to dinner. The Emperor was very kind and amiable to her, and she seemed to be much better. Everything points to the Empress being more happy in her new position, and we also.' On this Christmas Day Napoleon had his last meal with Josephine.

~ 168 ~

To The Empress, at Malmaison.

Paris, Wednesday, noon, 27th December 1809.

Eugène told me that you were very miserable all yesterday. That is not well, my dear; it is contrary to what you promised me. I have been thoroughly tired in revisiting the Tuileries; that great palace seemed empty to me and I felt lost in it.

Adieu, dear. Keep well.

Napoleon

~ 169 ~

To The Empress, at Malmaison.

Paris, Sunday, December 31, 10 a.m., 1809.

My Dear,

Today I have a Grand parade; I shall see all my Old Guard and more than sixty pieces of artillery.

The King of Westphalia is returning home, which will leave a house vacant in Paris. I am sad not to see you. If the parade finishes before 3 o'clock, I will come; otherwise, tomorrow.

Adieu, dear.

Napoleon

~ 170 ~

To The Empress, at Malmaison.

Thursday Evening, 1810.

My Dear,

Hortense, whom I saw this afternoon, has given me news of you. I trust that you will have been able to see your plants today, the weather having been fine. I have only been out for a few minutes at three o'clock to shoot some hares.

Adieu, dear; sleep well.

Napoleon

Thursday, January 4th.

Hortense. – *Louis had tried to obtain a divorce. Cambacérès was ordered on December 22nd to summon a family council (*New Letters of Napoleon I, *No. 234); but the wish of the King was refused (verbally, says Louis in his* Historical Documents of Holland*), whereupon he refused to agree to Josephine's divorce, but had to give way, and was present at what he calls the farewell festival given by the city of Paris to the Empress Josephine on January 1st. The ecclesiastical divorce was pronounced on January 12th.*

~ 171 ~

To The Empress, at Malmaison.

Friday, 8 p.m., 1810.

I wished to come and see you today, but I cannot; it will be, I hope, in the morning. It is a long time since I heard from you. I learnt with pleasure that you take walks in your garden these cold days.

Adieu, dear; keep well, and never doubt my affection.

Napoleon

January 5th. He duly visits Josephine the next day.

~ 172 ~

To The Empress, at Malmaison.

Sunday, 8 p.m., 1810.

I was very glad to see you yesterday; I feel what charms your society has for me.

Today I walked with Estève. I have allowed £4,000 for 1810, for the extraordinary expenses at Malmaison. You can therefore do as much planting as you like; you will distribute that sum as you may require. I have instructed Estève to send £8,000 the moment the contract for the Maison Julien shall be made. I have ordered them to pay for your *parure* of rubies, which will be valued by the Department, for I do not wish to be robbed by jewellers. So, there goes the £16,000 that this may cost me.

I have ordered them to hold the million which the Civil List owes you for 1810 at the disposal of your accountant, in order to pay your debts.

You should find in the coffers of Malmaison twenty to twenty-five thousand pounds; you can take them to buy your plate and linen.

I have instructed them to make you a very fine porcelain service; they will take your commands in order that it may be a very fine one.

January 7th is the date.

What charms your society has. – *Her repertoire of small talk and scandal. This long kind letter was doubtless intended to be specially so, for two days later the clergy of Paris pronounced the annulment of her marriage. This was far worse than the pronouncement by the Senate in December as it meant to her that she and Napoleon had never been properly married at all. The Emperor, who hated divorces, and especially* divorcées, *had found great difficulty in breaking down the barriers he had helped to build, for which purpose* he *had to be subordinated to his own Senate. Seven bishops allowed the annulment of the marriage, held in 1804 before the coronation, on account of (1) its secrecy, (2) the insufficiency of consent of the contracting parties, and (3) the absence of the local parish priest at the ceremony. The last reason was merely a technical one.*

~ 173 ~

To The Empress, at Malmaison.

Wednesday, 6 p.m., 1810.

My Dear,

I see no objection to your receiving the King of Westphalia whenever you wish. The King and Queen of Bavaria will probably come to see you on Friday.

I long to come to Malmaison, but you must really show fortitude and self-restraint; the page on duty this morning told me that he saw you weeping.

I am going to dine quite alone.

Adieu, dear. Never doubt the depth of my feelings for you; you would be unjust and unfair if you did.

Napoleon

Wednesday, January 10th.

King of Westphalia. – *Napoleon's brother, Jerome. Madame Durand (*Napoleon and Marie Louise*) says that, forced to abandon his wife (the beautiful and energetic Miss Paterson) and child, Jerome 'had vowed he would never sleep with a wife who had been forced upon him'. For three years he lavished his attentions upon almost all the beauties of the Westphalian court. The queen, an eyewitness of this conduct, bore it with mild and forbearing dignity. Then, one night, the right wing of the palace of Cassel, in which the queen's apartments were situated, caught fire; alarmed by the screams of her women the queen awoke and sprang out of her bed, to be caught in the arms of the king and carried to a place of safety. From that time forth the royal couple were united and happy.*

~ 174 ~

To The Empress, at Malmaison.

Saturday, 1 p.m., 1810.

My Dear,

Yesterday I saw Eugène, who told me that you gave a reception to the kings. I was at the concert till eight o'clock, and only dined, quite alone, at that hour.

I long to see you. If I do not come today, I will come after mass.

Adieu, dear. I hope to find you sensible and in good health. This weather should indeed make you put on flesh.

Saturday, January 13th.

Sensible. – *This was now possible after a month's mourning. At first, according to Madame Rémusat, her mind often wandered. But Napoleon himself encouraged the Court to visit her, and the road to Malmaison was soon a crowded one. As the days passed, however, life became sadly monotonous. Reading palled on Josephine, as did whist and the daily feeding of her golden pheasants and guinea-fowls.*

~ 175 ~

To The Empress, at Malmaison.

Trianon, January 17, 1810.

My Dear,

D'Audenarde, whom I sent to you this morning, tells me that since you have been at Malmaison you have no longer any courage. Yet that place is full of our happy memories, which can and ought never to change, at least on my side.

I want badly to see you, but I must have some assurance that you are strong and not weak; I too am rather like you, and it makes me frightfully wretched.

Adieu, Josephine; good-night. If you doubted me, you would be very ungrateful.

D'Audenarde. – *Napoleon's handsome equerry, whom Mlle. d'Avrillon calls* 'un homme superbe'. *His mother was Josephine's favourite* dame du palais. *Madame Lalaing, Viscountess D'Audenarde,* née *Peyrac, was one of the old regime who had been ruined by the Revolution.*

~ 176 ~

To The Empress, at Malmaison.

January 20, 1810.

My Dear,

I send you the box that I promised you the day before yesterday – representing the Island of Lobau. I was rather tired yesterday. I work much, and do not go out.

Adieu, dear.

Napoleon

~ 177 ~

To The Empress, at Malmaison.

Noon, Tuesday, 1810.

I hear that you are making yourself miserable; this is too bad. You have no confidence in me, and all the rumours that are being spread strike you; this is not knowing me, Josephine. I am much annoyed, and if I do not find you cheerful and contented, I shall scold you a great deal.

Adieu, dear.

Napoleon

Tuesday, January 23rd.

On January 21st a Privy Council was summoned to approve of Marie Louise as their 'choice of a consort, who may give an heir to the throne' (Thiers). Cambacérès, Fouché, and Murat wished for the Russian princess; Lebrun, Cardinal Fesch and King Louis for a Saxon one; but Talleyrand, Champagny, Maret, Berthier and Fontanes were for Austria.

~ 178 ~

To The Empress, at Malmaison.

Sunday, January 28, 9 p.m., 1810.

My Dear,

I was very glad to see you the day before yesterday.

I hope to go to Malmaison during the week. I have had all your affairs looked after here, and ordered that everything be brought to the Élysée-Napoleon.

Please take care of yourself.

Adieu, dear.

Napoleon

~ 179 ~

To The Empress, at Malmaison.

January 30, 1810.

My Dear,

Your letter to hand. I hope the walk you had yesterday, in order to show people your conservatories, has done you good.

I will gladly see you at the Élysée, and shall be very glad to see you more often, for you know how I love you.

Napoleon

Josephine had heard she was to be banished from Paris, and so had asked to come to the Élysée to prove the truth or otherwise of the rumour.

L'Élysée. – *Having, under the Revolution, become national property, it had been hired by the caterers of public entertainments, who gave it the name of L'Élysée. In 1803 it became the property of Murat, who, becoming King of Naples, ceded it to Napoleon in 1808. Here Napoleon signed his second abdication, here resided Alexander I in 1815, and here Josephine's grandson effected the* Coup d'État *(1851). When the Senatus Consultus fixed the revenue of Josephine, Napoleon not only gave her whatever rights he had in Malmaison, i.e., at least 90 per cent of the total cost, but the palace of the Élysée, its gardens and dependencies, with the furniture then in use. The latter residence was, however, for her life only.*

~ 180 ~

To The Empress, at Malmaison.

Saturday, 6 p.m., 1810.

I told Eugène that you would rather listen to the vulgar gossip of a great city than to what I told you; yet people should not be allowed to invent fictions to make you miserable.

I have had all your effects moved to the Élysée. You should come to Paris at once; but be at ease and contented, and have full confidence in me.

Napoleon

~ 181 ~

To The Empress, at the Élysée-Napoleon.

February 19, 1810.

My Dear,

I have received your letter. I long to see you, but the reflections that you make may be true. It is, perhaps, not desirable that we should be under the same roof for the first year. Yet Bessières' country-house is too far off to go and return in one day; in any case I have a bad cold, and am not sure of being able to go there.

Adieu, dear.

Napoleon

~ 182 ~

To The Empress, at Élysée-Napoleon.

Friday, 6 p.m., 1810.

Savary, as soon as he arrived, brought me your letter; I am sorry to see you are unhappy. I am very glad that you saw nothing of the fire.

I had fine weather at Rambouillet.

Hortense told me that you had some idea of coming to a dinner at Bessières', and of returning to Paris to sleep. I am sorry that you have not been able to manage it.

Adieu, dear. Be cheerful, and consider how much you please me thereby.

Napoleon

Rambouillct. – *He had taken the Court with him, and was there from February 19th to the 23rd, the date of this letter. While there he had been in the best of humours. On his return he finds it necessary to write to his future wife and to her father – and to pen a legible letter to the latter gives him far more trouble than winning a battle against the Austrians.*

Adieu. – *Sick and weary, Josephine returns to Malmaison, Friday, March 9th, and even this is not long to be hers, for the new Empress is almost already on her way. The marriage at Vienna took place on March 11th, with her uncle Charles, the hero of Essling, for Napoleon's proxy (on this occasion Baron Lejeune sees the Archduke Charles and remarks: "There was nothing in his quiet face with its grave and gentle expression, or in his simple, modest, unassuming manner, to denote the mighty man of war; but no one who met his eyes could doubt him to be a genius"); on the 13th she leaves Vienna, and on the 23rd reaches Strasburg. On the 27th she meets Napoleon at Compiègne, spends three days with him in the château there, and arrives at St. Cloud on April 1st, where the civil marriage is renewed, followed by the triumphal entry into Paris, and the religious ceremony on April 2nd. This day Josephine reaches the château of Navarre.*

The marriage of Napoleon to the young Archduchess of Austria, Marie Louise.

~ 183 ~

To The Empress, at Malmaison.

March 12, 1810.

My Dear,

I trust that you will be pleased with what I have done for Navarre. You must see from that how anxious I am to make myself agreeable to you.

Get ready to take possession of Navarre; you will go there on March 25th, to pass the month of April.

Adieu, dear.

Napoleon

~ 183A ~

Letter of the Empress Josephine
To The Emperor Napoleon
Navarre, April 19, 1810.
Sire,
I have received, by my son, the assurance that your Majesty consents to my return to Malmaison, and grants to me the advances asked for in order to make the château of Navarre habitable. This double favour, Sire, dispels to a great extent the uneasiness, nay, even the fears which your Majesty's long silence had inspired. I was afraid that I might be entirely banished from your memory; I see that I am not. I am therefore less wretched today, and even as happy as it will be possible for me to be.

I shall go at the end of the month to Malmaison, since your Majesty sees no objection to it. But I ought to tell you, Sire, that I should not so soon have taken advantage of the latitude which your Majesty left me in this respect had the house of Navarre not required, for my health's sake and for that of my household, repairs which are urgent. My idea is to stay at Malmaison a very short time; I shall soon leave it in order to go to the waters. But while I am at Malmaison, your Majesty may be sure that I shall live there as if I were a thousand leagues from Paris. I have made a great sacrifice, Sire, and every day I realise more its full extent. Yet that sacrifice will be, as it ought to be, a complete one on my part. Your Highness, amid your happiness, shall be troubled by no expression of my regret.

I shall pray unceasingly for your Majesty's happiness, perhaps even I shall pray that I may see you again; but your Majesty may be assured that I shall always respect our new relationship. I shall respect it in silence, relying on the attachment that you had to me formerly; I shall call for no new proof; I shall trust to everything from your justice and your heart.

I limit myself to asking from you one favour: it is, that you will deign to find a way of sometimes convincing both myself and my entourage that I have still a small place in your memory and a great place in your esteem and friendship. By this means, whatever happens, my sorrows will be mitigated without, as it seems to me, compromising that which is of permanent importance to me, the happiness of your Majesty.

Josephine

Navarre. – *In February 1810, Napoleon determined to purchase this château. The old square building was, however, utterly unfit to be inhabited. No wonder if her household, banished to such a place, sixty-five miles from Paris, should rebel. Whist and piques soon grow stale in such a house and with such surroundings, and even* trictrac *with the old bishop of Evreux becomes tedious. Eugène as usual brings sunshine in his path, and helps to dispel the gloom caused by the idle gossip imported from Paris – that Josephine is not to return to Malmaison, and the like. This was Josephine's second letter, says D'Avrillon, the first being answered* vivâ voce *by Eugène.*

To Malmaison. – *Napoleon had promised Josephine permission to return to Malmaison, and would not recant: his new wife was, however, very jealous of Josephine, and very much hurt at her presence at Malmaison. Napoleon managed to be away from Paris for six weeks after Josephine's arrival at Malmaison.*

~ 184 ~

(Reply of the Emperor Napoleon to the preceding.)

To The Empress Josephine, at Navarre.

Compiègne, April 21, 1810.

My Dear,

I have yours of April 19th; it is written in a bad style. I am always the same; people like me do not change. I don't know what Eugène has told you. I have not written to you because you have not written to me, and my sole desire is to fulfil your slightest inclination.

I see with pleasure that you are going to Malmaison and that you are contented; as for me, I shall be so likewise on hearing news from you and in giving you mine. I say no more about it until you have compared this letter with yours, and after that I will leave you to judge which of us two is the better friend.

Adieu, dear; keep well, and be just for your sake and mine.

Napoleon

~ 184A ~

Reply of the Empress Josephine.

A thousand, thousand loving thanks for not having forgotten me. My son has just brought me your letter. With what impetuosity I read it, and yet I took a long time over it, for there was not a word which did not make me weep; but these tears were very pleasant ones. I have found my whole heart again – such as it will always be; there are affections which are life itself, and which can only end with it.

I was in despair to find my letter of the 19th had displeased you; I do not remember the exact expressions, but I know what torture I felt in writing it – the grief at having no news from you.

I wrote to you on my departure from Malmaison, and since then how often have I wished to write to you! But I appreciated the causes of your silence and feared to be importunate with a letter. Yours has been such a relief for me. Be happy, be as much so as you deserve; it is my whole heart which speaks to you. You have also just given me my share of happiness, and a share which I value the most, for nothing can equal in my estimation a proof that you still remember me.

Adieu, dear; I again thank you as affectionately as I shall always love you.

Josephine

This letter seems to have been taken by Eugène to Paris, and from there forwarded to the Emperor with a letter from that Prince in which he enumerates Josephine's suggestions and wishes – (1) that she will not go to Aix-la-Chapelle if other waters are suggested by Corvisart; (2) that after stopping a few days at Malmaison she will go in June for three months to the baths, and afterwards to the south of France; visit Rome, Florence, and Naples incognito, spend the winter at Milan, and return to Malmaison and Navarre in the spring of 1811; (3) that in her absence the Château of Navarre shall be made habitable, for which fresh funds are required; (4) that Josephine wishes her cousins the Taschers to marry, one a relative of King Joseph, the other the Princess Amelie de la Leyen, niece of the Prince Primate. To this Napoleon replies from Compiègne, April 26th, that the De Leyen match with Louis Tascher may take place (he endows the husband with £4,000 a year, and the title of Count Tascher), but that he will not interest himself in the other (Henry) Tascher, who is giddy-headed and bad-tempered. 'I consent to whatever the Empress does, but I will not confer any mark of my regard on a person who has behaved ill to me. I am very glad that the Empress likes Navarre. I am giving orders to have £12,000 which I owe her for 1810, and £12,000 for 1811 advanced to her. She will then have only the £80,000 from the public treasury to come in ... She is free to go to whatever spa she cares for, and even to return to Paris afterwards.' He thinks, however, she would be happier in new places which they had never visited together, as they had Aix-la-Chapelle. If, however, the last are the best she may go to them, for 'what I desire above all is that she may keep calm, and not allow herself to be excited by the gossip of Paris.'

~ 185 ~

To The Empress Josephine, at the Château Navarre.

Compiègne, April 28, 1810.

My Dear,

I have just received two letters from you. I am writing to Eugène. I have ordered that the marriage of Tascher with the Princess de la Leyen can take place.

Tomorrow I shall go to Antwerp to see my fleet and to give orders about the works. I shall return on May 15th.

Eugène tells me that you wish to go to the waters; trouble yourself about nothing. Do not listen to the gossip of Paris; it is idle and far from knowing the real state of things. My feelings for you do not change, and I would really like to know that you are happy and content.

Napoleon

Two letters. – *The other, now missing, may have some reference to the pictures to which he refers in his letter to Fouché the next day. 'Is it true that engravings are being published with the title of* Josephine Beauharnais née La Pagerie? *If this is true, have the prints seized, and let the engravers be punished (*New Letters, *No. 253).*

~ 186 ~

To The Empress Josephine, at Malmaison.

My Dear,

I have your letter. Eugène will give you news of my journey and of the Empress. I am very glad that you are going to the spa. I trust it will do you good.

I wish very much to see you. If you are at Malmaison at the end of the month, I will come to see you. I expect to be at St. Cloud on the 30th of the month My health is very good… I only need to hear that you are content and well. Let me know in what name you intend to travel.

Never doubt the whole truth of my affection for you; it will last as long as I. You would be very unjust if you doubted it.

Napoleon

Probably written from Boulogne about May 25th. His northern tour with Marie Louise had been very similar to one taken in 1804, but his entourage found the new bride very cold and distant compared to Josephine. Leaving Paris on April

29th Napoleon's Correspondence till June is dated Lacken (April 30th); Antwerp (May 3rd); Bois-le-Duc; Middleburg, Ghent, Bruges, Ostend (May 20th); Lille, Boulogne, Dieppe, Le Havre, Rouen (May 31st). He takes the Empress in a canal barge from Brussels to Malines and himself descends the subterranean vault of the Scheldt-Oise canal, between St. Quentin and Cambrai. He is at St. Cloud on June 2nd.

Josephine has felt his wanderings less, as she has the future Emperor Napoleon III, her favourite grandson, with her, the little Oui-Oui, as she calls him, and for whom the damp spring weather of Holland was dangerous. She was also at Malmaison from the middle of May to June 18th. The original collection of Letters (Didot Frères, 1833) heads the letter correctly to the Empress Josephine at Malmaison, but the Correspondence, *published by order of Napoleon III, gives it erroneously, to the Empress Josephine,* at the Château of Navarre *(No. 16,537).*

I will come to see you. – *He comes for two hours on June 13th, and makes himself thoroughly agreeable. Poor Josephine is light-headed with joy all the evening after. The meeting of the two Empresses is, however, indefinitely postponed, and Josephine had now no further reason to delay her departure. Leaving her little grandson Louis behind, she travels under the name of the Countess d'Arberg, and she is accompanied by Madame D'Audenarde and Mlle. de Mackau, who left the Princess Stephanie to come to Navarre. They go via Lyons and Geneva to Aix-les-Bains. M. Masson, who made a careful and complete study of this period, describes the daily round. 'Josephine, on getting out of bed, takes conscientiously her baths and showers, then, as usual, lies down again until déjeuner, 11 a.m., for which the whole of the little Court are assembled at* The Palace *– wherever she lives, and however squalid the dwelling-place, her abode always bears this name. Afterwards she and her women-folk ply their interminable tapestry, while the latest novel or play (sent by Barbier from Paris) is read aloud. And so the day passes till five, when they dress for dinner at six; after dinner a ride. At nine the Empress's friends assemble in her room, Mlle. de Mackau sings; at eleven every one goes to bed.'*

~ 187 ~

To The Empress Josephine, at the Waters of Aix, in Savoy.

Rambouillet, July 8, 1810.

My Dear,

I have your letter of July 8th. You will have seen Eugène, and his presence will have done you good. I learn with pleasure that the waters are beneficial to you. The King of Holland has just abdicated the throne, whilst leaving the Regency, according to the Constitution, in the hands of the Queen. He has quitted Amsterdam and left the Grand Duke of Berg behind.

I have reunited Holland to France, which has, however, the advantage of setting the Queen at liberty, and that unfortunate girl is coming to Paris with her son the Grand Duke of Berg – that will make her perfectly happy.

My health is good. I have come here to hunt for a few days. I shall see you this autumn with pleasure. Never doubt my friendship; I never change.

Keep well, be cheerful, and believe in the truth of my attachment.

Napoleon

July 8th. – *On July 5th, driving along the Chambéry road, Josephine met the courier with a letter from Eugène describing the terrible fire at Prince Schwartzenberg's ball, where the Princess de la Leyen died. It is noteworthy that the Emperor makes no allusion to the conflagration. As, however, this is the first letter since the end of May, others may have been lost or destroyed.*

You will have seen Eugène. – *i.e. on his way to Milan, who arrived at Aix on July 10th. He had just been made heir to the Grand Duchy of Frankfurt – a broad hint to him and to Europe that Italy would be eventually united to France under Napoleon's dynasty. This was the nadir of the Beauharnais family – Josephine divorced, Hortense lost her throne and unwed, and Eugène's expectations dissipated, and all within a few short months. Eugène had left his wife ill at Geneva, where Josephine goes to visit her the next day. Geneva was always the home of the disaffected, and so the Empress had to be specially tactful, and the De Rémusat reports: 'She speaks of the Emperor as of a brother, of the new Empress as the one who will give children to France, and if the rumours of the latter's condition be correct, I am certain she will be delighted about it.'*

That unfortunate daughter is coming to France. – *i.e. to reside when she is not at St. Leu (given to her by Napoleon) or at the waters. On the present occasion she has been at Plombières a month or more. On July 10th Napoleon instructs the Countess de Boubers to bring the Grand Duke of Berg to Paris, 'whom he awaits with impatience ' (*Brotonne, *625).*

~ 188 ~

To The Empress Josephine, at the Waters of Aix, in Savoy.

St. Cloud, July 20, 1810.

My Dear,

I have received your letter of July 14th, and note with pleasure that the waters are doing you good, and that you like Geneva. I think that you are doing well to go there for a few weeks.

My health is fairly good. The conduct of the King of Holland has worried me.

Hortense is shortly coming to Paris. The Grand Duke of Berg is on his way; I expect him tomorrow.

Adieu, dear.

Napoleon

The conduct of the King of Holland has worried me. – *On May 20th he had written to Louis that he must 'Before all things be a Frenchman and the Emperor's brother and then you may be sure you are in the path of the true interests of Holland. Good sense and policy are necessary to the government of states, not sour unhealthy bile.' And three days later: 'Write me no more of your customary twaddle; three years now it has been going on, and every instant proves its falsehood! This is the last letter I shall ever write you in my life.' Louis at one time determined on war, and rather than surrender Amsterdam, to cut the dykes. The Emperor hears of this, summons his brother, and practically imprisons him until he countermands the defence of Amsterdam. On July 1st Louis abdicated and fled to Toeplitz in Bohemia. Napoleon is terribly grieved at the conduct of his brother, who would never agree that the Continental blockade could force peace upon England.*

~ 189 ~

To The Empress Josephine, at the Waters of Aix, in Savoy.

Trianon, August 10, 1810.

Your letter to hand. I was pained to see what a risk you had run. For an inhabitant of the isles of the ocean to die in a lake would have been a fatality indeed!

The Queen is better, and I hope her health will be re-established. Her husband is in Bohemia, apparently not knowing what to do.

I am fairly well, and beg you to believe in my sincere attachment.

Napoleon

To die in a lake. – *i.e. the Lake of Bourget, where a storm had nearly capsized the sailing boat. Josephine had been on a visit to the Haute-Combe abbey on July 26th and the storm had overtaken her on the return voyage.*

~ 190 ~

To The Empress Josephine, at the Waters of Aix, in Savoy.

St. Cloud, September 14, 1810.

My Dear,

I have your letter of September 9th. I learn with pleasure that you keep well. There is no longer the slightest doubt that the Empress has entered on the fourth month of her pregnancy; she is well, and is much attached to me. The young Princes Napoleon are very well; they are in the Pavillon d'Italie, in the Park of St. Cloud.

Napoleon at St. Cloud with the children of Hortense and Caroline. On his knee is the future Napoleon III.

My health is fairly good. I wish to learn that you are happy and contented. I hear that one of your *entourage* has broken a leg while going on the glacier.

Adieu, dear. Never doubt the interest I take in you and the affection that I bear towards you.

Napoleon

~ 191 ~

To The Empress, at Malmaison.

Paris, this Friday.

My Dear,

Yours to hand. I am sorry to see that you have been ill; I fear it must be this bad weather.

Madame de la T. is one of the most foolish women of the Faubourg. I have borne her cackle for a very long time; I am sick of it, and have ordered that she does not come again to Paris. There are five or six other old women that I equally wish to send away from Paris; they are spoiling the young ones by their follies.

I will name Madame de Mackau Baroness since you wish it, and carry out your other commissions.

My health is pretty good. The conduct of B. appears to me very ridiculous. I trust to hear that you are better.

Adieu, dear.

Napoleon

Paris, this Friday. – *A very valuable note of M. Masson (*Josephine Répudiée, *198) enables us to fix this letter at its correct date. He says: 'It has to do with the exile of Madame de la T. (the Princess Louis de la Trémoille), which takes place on September 28th, 1810, and this 28th September is also a Friday: there is also the question of Mlle. de Mackau being made a baroness' (and this lady had not joined the Court of Josephine till May 1810); 'lastly, the B. mentioned therein can only be Barante, the Prefect, whose dismissal (from Geneva) almost coincides with this letter.' It may be added that the La Trémoille family was one of the oldest in France, allied with the Condés, and consequently with the Bourbons. Barante's fault had been connivance at the letters and conduct of Madame de Staël.*

~ 192 ~

To The Empress Josephine, at Geneva.

Fontainebleau, October 1, 1810.

I have received your letter. Hortense, whom I have seen, will have told you what I think. Go to see your son this winter; come back to the waters of Aix next year, or, still better, wait for the spring at Navarre. I would advise you to go to Navarre at once, if I did not fear you would get tired of it. In my view, the only suitable places for you this winter are either Milan or Navarre; after that, I approve of whatever you may do, for I do not wish to vex you in anything.

Adieu, dear. The Empress is as I told you in my last letter. I am naming Madame de Montesquieu governess of the Children of France. Be contented, and do not get excited; never doubt my affection for you.

The only suitable places... are either Milan or Navarre. – *Milan had been her own suggestion conveyed by Eugène, but Napoleon, two months later, had told her she could spend the winter in France, and in spite of danger signals from Madame de Rémusat (in her fulsome and tedious 'despatch' sent from Paris in September, and probably inspired by the Emperor himself) she manages to get to Navarre, and even to spend the first fortnight of November at Malmaison. Before leaving Switzerland Josephine refuses to risk an interview with Madame de Staël. 'In the first book she publishes she will not fail to report our conversation, and heaven knows how many things she will make me say that I have never even thought of.'*

~ **193** ~

To The Empress Josephine, at Navarre.
Fontainebleau, November 14, 1810.
My Dear,
I have received your letter. Hortense has spoken to me about it. I note with pleasure that you are contented. I hope that you are not very tired of Navarre.

My health is very good. The Empress progresses satisfactorily. I will do the various things you ask regarding your household. Take care of your health, and never doubt my affection for you.

Napoleon

In spite of the heading Josephine was at Malmaison on this day, and Napoleon writes to Cambacérès: 'My cousin, the Empress Josephine is not leaving for Navarre till Monday or Tuesday, I wish you to pay her a visit. You will let me know on your return how you find her ' (Brotonne, *721). The real reason is to hasten her departure, and she gets to Navarre by November 22nd (Thursday).*

The Empress progresses satisfactorily. – *Napoleon writes to her father, the Emperor of Austria, on the same day: 'The Empress is very well ... It is impossible that the wife for whom I am indebted to you should be more perfect. Moreover, I beg your Majesty to rest assured that she and I are equally attached to you.'*

~ 194 ~

To The Empress Josephine, at Navarre.

I havc your letter. I see no objection to the marriage of Mackau with Wattier, if he wishes it; this general is a very brave man. I am in good health I hope to have a son; I shall let you know immediately.

Adieu, dear. I am very glad that Madame d'Arberg has told you things which please you. When you see me, you will find me with my old affection for you.

Napoleon

Madame d'Arberg. – *Josephine's chief maid-of-honour.*

~ 195 ~

To The Empress Josephine, at Navarre.

Paris, January 8th, 1811.

I have your New Year's letter. I thank you for its contents. I note with pleasure that you are well and happy. I hear that there are more women than men at Navarre.

My health is excellent, though I have not been out for a fortnight. Eugène appears to have no fears about his wife; he gives you a grandson.

Adieu, dear; keep well.

Napoleon

Napoleon's son, the King of Rome, is baptised on June 9th, 1811.

~ 196 ~

To The Empress Josephine, at Navarre.

Paris, March 22nd, 1811.

My Dear,

I have your letter. I thank you for it.

My son is fat, and in excellent health. I trust he may continue to improve. He has my chest, my mouth, and my eyes. I hope he may fulfil his destiny. I am always well pleased with Eugène; he has never given me the least anxiety.

Napoleon

There is a full account of the birth of the King of Rome in Napoleon's letter to the Emperor of Austria on March 20th (No. 17,496). The letter of this date to

Josephine is missing, but is referred to by D'Avrillon. It began, 'My dear Josephine, I have a son. I am stricken with happiness.'

Eugène. – *Josephine much appreciated this allusion. 'Is it possible', she said, 'for any one to be kinder than the Emperor, and more anxious to mitigate whatever might be painful for me at the present moment, if I loved him less sincerely? This association of my son with his own is well worthy of him who, when he likes, is the most fascinating of all men.' She gave a costly ring to the page who brought the letter.*

On the previous day Eugène had arrived at Navarre, sent by the Emperor. 'You are going to see your mother, Eugène; tell her I am sure that she will rejoice more than any one at my happiness. I should have already written to her if I had not been absorbed by the pleasure of watching my boy. The moments I snatch from his side are only for matters of urgent necessity. This event, I shall acquit myself of the most pleasant of them all by writing to Josephine.'

~ **197** ~

To The Empress Josephine, at Malmaison.

Trianon, August 25th, 1811.

I have your letter. I see with pleasure that you are in good health. I have been for some days at Trianon. I expect to go to Compiègne. My health is very good.

Put some order into your affairs. Spend only £60,000, and save as much every year; that will make a sum of £600,000 in ten years for your grandchildren. It is pleasant to be able to give them something, and be helpful to them. Instead of that, I hear you have debts, which would be really too bad. Look after your affairs, and don't give to every one who wants to help himself. If you wish to please me, let me hear that you have accumulated a large fortune. Consider how ill I must think of you, if I know that you, with £125,000 a year, are in debt.

Adieu, dear; keep well.

Napoleon

Josephine in 1810.

The last portrait of Josephine.

~ 198 ~

To The Empress Josephine, at Malmaison.

Friday, 8 a.m., 1811.

I send to know how you are, for Hortense tells me you were in bed yesterday. I was annoyed with you about your debts. I do not wish you to have any; on the contrary, I wish you to put a million aside every year, to give to your grandchildren when they get married.

Nevertheless, never doubt my affection for you, and don't worry any more about the present embarrassment.

Adieu, dear. Send me word that you are well. They say that you are as fat as a good Normandy farm wife.

Napoleon

Written in November 1811.

As fat as a good Normandy farm wife. – *Madame d'Abrantes, who saw her about this time, writes: 'I observed that Josephine had grown very stout since the time of my departure for Spain. This change was at once for the better and the worse. It imparted a more youthful appearance to her face; but her slender and elegant figure, which had been one of her principal attractions, had entirely disappeared. She had now decided* embonpoint, *and her figure had assumed that matronly air which we find in the statues of Agrippina, Cornelia, etc. Still, however, she looked uncommonly well, and she wore a dress which became her admirably. Her judicious taste in these matters contributed to make her appear young much longer than she otherwise would. The best proof of the admirable taste of Josephine is the marked absence of elegance shown by Marie Louise, though both Empresses employed the same milliners and dressmakers, and Marie Louise had a large sum allotted for the expenses of her wardrobe.'*

Mlle d'Avrillon says that during the Swiss voyage Josephine found it desirable for the first time, to 'wear whalebone in her corsets.'

~ 199 ~

To The Empress Josephine, at Malmaison.

June 12th, 1812.

My Dear,

I shall always receive news from you with great interest.

The waters will, I hope, do you good, and I shall see you with much pleasure on your return.

Never doubt the interest I feel in you. I will arrange all the matters of which you speak.

Napoleon

Written from Königsberg (M. Masson, in Josephine Répudiée, *says Danzig; but on June 11th Napoleon writes to Eugène, 'I shall be at Königsberg tomorrow', where his correspondence is dated from now on). A day or two later he writes to the King of Rome's governess that he trusts to hear soon that the fifteen months old child has cut his first four teeth.*

~ 200 ~

To The Empress Josephine, at Malmaison.

Gumbinnen, June 20th, 1812.

I have your letter of June 10th. I see no obstacle to your going to Milan, to be near the Vicereine. You will do well to go *incognito*. You will find it very hot.

My health is very good. Eugène is well, and is doing good work. Never doubt the interest I have in you, and my friendship.

Napoleon

Gumbinnen, June 20th. – *Just a few days before Napoleon's massive army crosses the Niemen into Russian territory.*

Josephine meanwhile has permission to go to Italy. Owing to her grandson's illness she defers starting till July 16th. Through frightful weather she reaches Milan via Geneva on July 28th, and has a splendid reception. On the 29th she writes to Hortense: 'I have found the three letters from Eugène, the last one dated the 13th; his health is excellent. He still pursues the Russians, without being able to overtake them. It is generally hoped the campaign may be a short one. May that hope be realised!'. Two days later she announces the birth of Eugène's daughter Amelia, afterwards Empress of Brazil. Towards the end of August Josephine goes to Aix and meets Joseph Bonaparte's wife, the Queen of Spain, with her sister Desirée Bernadotte, the former 'kind and amiable as usual', the latter 'very gracious to me' – rather a new experience. From Aix she goes to Prégny-la-Tour, on the Lake of Geneva. She gets to Malmaison on October 24th. Soon after his return from Moscow Napoleon pays her a visit, and about this time she sees the infant King of Rome, whose mother has always thought more of her daily music and drawing lessons than of whether she was making her son happy or not. 1812 closed in gloom, but 1813 was, if anything, just as bad.

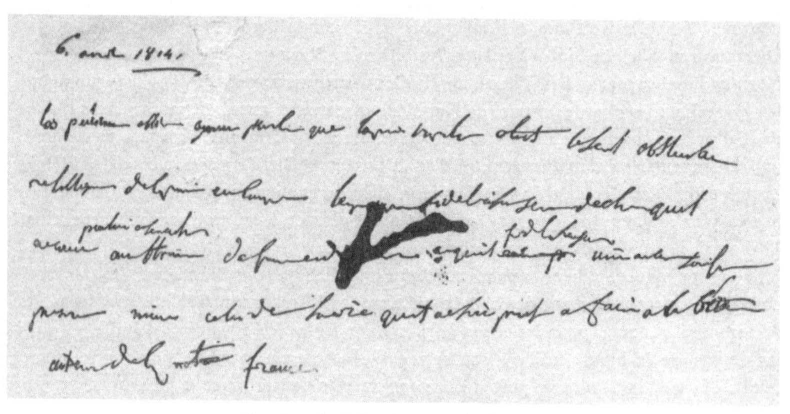
6. avril 1814.

Napoleon's abdication, April 6th 1814.

Up to August Fortune had smiled again upon her favourite. But weight of numbers and incompetence had undermined the Empire, and Leipzig (that battle of giants, where 110,000 soldiers were killed and wounded) made final success hopeless.

In 1814 the Allies invade France. Meanwhile, Talleyrand is watching to guide the *coup de grâce*. Napoleon makes a dash for Lorraine to gather his garrisons and cut off the enemy's supplies. The Allies hesitate and are about to follow him, as per the rules of war, but, instead, make for Paris. Hortense in vain tries to keep Marie Louise in the capital, whose presence would have stimulated the Parisians, and thereby hold the Allies at bay.

After Marmont's betrayal Napoleon attempts suicide, and when he believes death imminent sends a last message to Josephine by Caulaincourt, 'You will tell Josephine that my thoughts were of her before life departed.' But he recovers and departs for Elba and exile instead.

It was on Monday, May 23rd, that Josephine's illness commenced, after receiving at dinner the King of Prussia and his sons. Whether the sore throat which killed her was a quinsy or diphtheria is difficult to prove, but the latter seems the more probable. Doctor Corvisart, who was himself ill and unable to attend, told Napoleon that she died of grief and worry. Before leaving for the

Waterloo campaign Napoleon visited Malmaison, and there, as Lord Rosebery reminds us, allowed his only oblique reproach to Marie Louise to escape him: 'Poor Josephine. Her death, of which the news took me by surprise at Elba, was one of the most acute griefs of that fatal year, 1814. She had her failings, of course; but she, at any rate, would never have abandoned me.'

1792
1795
Milan 1796
Egypte 1798
1804
Austerlitz 1805
Berlin 1806
Tilsit 1807
Madrid 1808
Schœnbrunn 1809
Dresde 1813
14 Juillet 1815
Erfurt 1813
Fontainebleau 1814
Ile d'Elbe 1814
Longwood 1816

Sixteen signitures of Napoleon between 1792 and 1816.

Provenance of the Letters

The major source for the early letters is Charles Tennant's collection published in 1824. Letters 1, 3, 4, 5, 6, 7 and 8 in the chapter The General were taken from this volume as was letter 3 in The Consul. Letter 2 in The General came from St. Amand's *La Citoyenne Bonaparte.*
More letters were collected and published by the Didot brothers in 1833. These were edited by Madame de Faverolles. Letters 9 to 22 and 24 to 33 of The General (letter 23 is from Bourrienne), all of The Consul (except letter 3) and all but letters 1, 5, 35 and 111 in The Emperor come from this source. Letter 1 is from the *Correspondance*, letter 5 from the collection of Baron Heath, letter 35 from D'Avrillon's collection, and 111 from Las Cases.

Many of the Didot Brothers' letters showed up later when Napoleon III had the vast *Correspondance de Napoleon I* published between 1858 and 1870.

The letters were translated by Henry Foljambe Hall in 1901 (published by J. M. Dent & Co. in London) but have been corrected and edited to appeal to a modern audience. Much of the archaic language has been altered and the supplementary notes have been edited, corrected and augmented.

Chronology

Napoleon as General

1796

March 11th – Bonaparte leaves Paris to join his army.
April 10th – Campaign opens (Napoleon's available troops about 35,000).
April 12th – Battle of Montenotte, Austrians defeated.
April 22nd. – Battle of Mondovi, Sardinians defeated.
April 28th – Armistice of Cherasco (submission of Sardinia to France): peace signed May 15th
May 8th – Austrians defeated at Fombio.
May 10th – passage of bridge of Lodi.
May 15th – Bonaparte enters Milan.
May 24th-25th – Revolt of Lombardy, and punishment of Pavia by the French.
May 30th-31st. – Bonaparte defeats Beaulieu at Borghetto.
June 3rd – Occupies Verona.
June 18th – Bonaparte enters Modena, and takes 50 cannon at Urbino.
June 19th – Occupies Bologna.
June 23rd – Armistice with Rome.
July 6th – Sortie from Mantua: Austrians fairly successful.
July 29th – advance of Wurmser.
July 31st. – Siege of Mantua raised.
August 3rd – Bonaparte victorious at Lonato.
August 5th – Augereau victorious at Castiglione.
September 8th – Battle of Bassano, Wurmser completely routed, and retires on Legnago.
September 13th – Wurmser reaches the suburbs of Mantua.
October 8th – Spain declares war against England.
October 10th – peace with Naples signed.
November 15th – First battle of Arcola. French gain partial victory.
November 16th and 17th – Second battle of Arcola. French completely victorious.
November 18th – Napoleon victoriously re-enters Verona.

1797

January 14th – Battle of Rivoli: Austrian centre defeated.
February 2nd. – Capitulation of Mantua, by Wurmser, with 13,000 men.
March 16th – Bonaparte defeats Archduke Charles on the Tagliamento.
April 17th – Preliminaries of peace at Leoben signed by Bonaparte.
September 4th – Day of 18th Fructidor at Paris. Coup d'État of Rewbell, Larévellière-Lépeaux, and Barras, secretly aided by Bonaparte.
October 17th – Treaty of Campo-Formio.
December 10th – Bonaparte presented to the Directory in Paris by Talleyrand.

1798

February 15th – Republic proclaimed at Rome.
May 20th – Napoleon sails from Toulon for Egypt.
July 21st. – Napoleon defeats Mamelukes at Battle of the Pyramids, and enters Cairo the following day.
September 12th – Turkey declares war on France.
December 15th – French occupy Rome.
December 29th – coalition of Russia, Austria, and England against France.

1799
June 22nd. – Turkey, Portugal, and Naples join the coalition against France.
August 23rd – Napoleon secretly sails for France.
October 9th – Napoleon lands at Frejus in France.
October 13th – Napoleon arrives at Paris.
November 9th – Napoleon dissolves the Directory and the next day the Council of Five Hundred.
December 24th Napoleon made First Consul.

NAPOLEON AS FIRST CONSUL

1800
May 6th – Napoleon leaves Paris.
June 2nd – Napoleon enters Milan, where he spends a week.
June 5th – Massena surrenders Genoa.
June 14th – Bonaparte wins Marengo.
June 16th – convention of Alessandria between Bonaparte and Melas.
July 3rd – the First Consul is back in Paris.
December 3rd – Moreau wins the battle of Hohenlinden
December 24th – Royalist conspirators fail to kill Bonaparte with an infernal machine.
1801
January 1st – Union of Great Britain and Ireland.
February 9th – Treaty of Luneville.
March 24th – The Czar Paul is assassinated.
April 2nd – Nelson bombards Copenhagen.
July 15th – Concordat between Bonaparte and the Pope.
October 8th – Treaty of Peace between France and Russia.
October 9th – And between France and Turkey.
December 14th – Expedition sent out to St. Domingo by the French under General Leclerc.
1802
January 4th – Louis Bonaparte marries Hortense Beauharnais, both unwilling.
March 25th – Treaty of Amiens signed in London.
August 2nd. – Napoleon Bonaparte made First Consul for life.
October 11th – Birth of Napoleon Charles, son of Louis Bonaparte and Hortense.
1803
April 30th -- France sells Louisiana to U.S. for £4,000,000 (15 million dollars).
May 22nd. – France declares war against England, chiefly respecting Malta.
1804
February 15th – The conspiracy of Pichegru. Moreau arrested.
March 21st – Duc D'Enghien shot.
May 18th – The First Consul becomes the Emperor Napoleon.

NAPOLEON AS EMPEROR

1804
December 2nd – Napoleon crowns himself Emperor, and Josephine Empress, in the presence and with the benediction of the Pope.
December 12th – Spain declares war against England.
1805
March 13th – Napoleon proclaimed King of Italy.
September 8th – Third Continental Coalition (Russia, Austria, and England against France).
September 24th – Napoleon leaves Paris.
October 17th – Capitulation of Ulm.
October 21st – Battle of Trafalgar; Franco-Spanish fleet destroyed after a five hours' fight.
November 13th – Vienna entered and bridge over the Danube seized. Massena crosses the Tagliamento.
December 2nd. – Battle of Austerlitz.
December 27th – Peace of Presburg.
1806
June 5th – Louis Bonaparte made King of Holland
July 12th – Napoleon forms Confederation of the Rhine, with himself as Chief and Protector.
October 8th – Prussia, assisted by Saxony, Russia, and England, declares war against France.

October 14th – Battles of Jena and Auerstadt.
October 25th – Marshal Davout enters Berlin.
November 28th – Murat enters Warsaw.

1807

February 8th – Battle of Eylau.
June 14th – Battle of Friedland, Napoleon defeats the Russian army.
July 7th – Peace signed between France and Russia.
November 22nd-25th – Napoleon at Milan.
December 17th – His Milan decree against English commerce.

1808

February 17th – French occupy Pamplona.
May 2nd – Murat subdues revolt at Madrid.
June 6th – King Joseph proclaimed King of Spain.
July 15th – Murat declared King of Naples.
July 22nd – Dupont capitulates at Baylen.
October 29th – English enter Spain.
November 4th – Napoleon enters Spain.
December 4th - Surrender of Madrid.

1809

January 17th – English army sails for England.
April 9th – Austrians under Archduke Charles enter Bavaria.
April 19th – Napoleon joins the army.
May 13th – French occupy Vienna.
May 21st–22nd. – Battle of Essling. A drawn battle.
July 5th-6th – Pope Pius VII carried off from Rome by order of Murat.
July 6th – Battle of Wagram.
October 14th – Treaty of Vienna, between France and Austria.
December 16th – French Senate pronounce the divorce of Napoleon and Josephine.

1810

January 9th – the clergy of Paris annul the religious marriage of Napoleon with Josephine.
February 7th – Convention of marriage between the Emperor Napoleon and the Archduchess Marie Louise.
April 1st – Civil marriage of Napoleon and Marie Louise.
July 1st – Louis Bonaparte, King of Holland, abdicates in favour of his son.
August 21st – Swedes elect Marshal Bernadotte Crown Prince of Sweden.

1811

March 20th – Birth of the King of Rome.

1812

May 9th – Napoleon leaves Paris for Germany.
June 24th – French cross the Niemen, over 450,000 strong.
August 12th – Wellington enters Madrid.
September 7th – Battle of Borodino.
September 14th – Occupation of Moscow.
October 19th – Commencement of the Retreat from Moscow.
December 5th – Napoleon reaches Smorgoni, and starts for France leaving the army behind.
December 18th – Napoleon reaches Paris.

1813

February 28th – Sixth Continental Coalition against France. Treaty signed between Russia and Prussia at Kalisch.
May 23rd – Duroc (shot on May 22nd) dies.
August 12th – Austria notifies its adhesion to the Allies.
October 7th – Wellington crosses the Bidassoa into France.
October 16th-19th – Battles of Leipzig.

1814

January 16th – Russians occupy Nancy.
January 19th – Austrians occupy Dijon.
January 29th – Combat of Brienne. Napoleon defeats Blucher.
March 29th – Allies outside Paris. Napoleon at Troyes (125 miles off).
March 30th – Battle of Paris. Napoleon reaches Fontainebleau in the evening, and hears the bad news.
March 31st – Emperor of Russia, King of Prussia, and 36,000 men enter Paris.
April 4th – Napoleon abdicates.
April 20th – Napoleon leaves for Elba.
May 29th – Death of Josephine, aged 51.